Miniature Gardens

BY ELVIN McDONALD

GROSSET
GOOD LIFE
BOOKS

PUBLISHERS • GROSSET & DUNLAP • NEW YORK

Cover photograph by Elvin McDonald

The author wishes to express his appreciation to the following for permission to use their illustrations in this book:

A & N Terrarium Company: p. 30, p. 31; Arthur E. Allgrove: p. 15; Anchor Hocking: p. 61, p. 68; Ralph Bailey: p. 53 bottom right, p. 74, p. 81 bottom, p. 82; Casa-Planta, Inc.: p. 85; Christen, Inc.: p. 44, p. 48; George Elbert: p. 88 top left, p. 88 bottom right; Fernwood Plants: p. 60 top, p. 63 bottom left, p. 64 bottom right; Fleco Industries: p. 84 bottom; George W. Park Seed Co., Inc.: p. 34 top, p. 40 top, p. 70 bottom, p. 70 top; Grigsby Cactus Gardens: p. 66 right; Henrietta's Nursery: p. 62 top, p. 63 top left, p. 63 top right, p. 63 middle right, p. 63 bottom right, p. 64 bottom left, p. 65 top, p. 65 middle, p. 66 left; Hort-Pix: p. 57 top, p. 78, p. 79, p. 80 top, p. 89; Jackson & Perkins Company: p. 58; Peter Kalberkamp, p. 73; Ward Linton: p. 52; Lord & Burnham Greenhouses: p. 86 top, p. 86 bottom, p. 87; Elvin McDonald: p. 8, p. 9, p. 16 top, p. 16 bottom, p. 17 top, p. 17 bottom, p. 18 top left, p. 18 top right, p. 18 bottom left, p. 18 bottom right, p. 28 top left, p. 28 top right, p. 28 bottom left, p. 34 middle, p. 34 bottom, p. 36 top, p. 36 middle, p. 36 bottom, p. 39, p. 40 bottom, p. 41 top, p. 41 middle, p. 41 bottom, p. 42 top, p. 42 middle, p. 42 bottom, p. 45 top, p. 45 middle, p. 45 bottom, p. 46 top, p. 46 middle, p. 46 bottom, p. 47, p. 49 bottom, p. 50 middle, p. 50 bottom, p. 51 bottom, p. 53 bottom left, p. 53 top right, p. 54 top, p. 54 middle, p. 54 bottom, p. 55 top, p. 55 middle, p. 55 bottom, p. 56 top, p. 56 middle, p. 56 bottom, p. 57 middle, p. 57 bottom, p. 60 middle, p. 60 bottom, p. 62 bottom, p. 64 top, p. 65 bottom, p. 67, p. 71, p. 77 right, p. 80 top, p. 80 bottom, p. 81 top, p. 84 top, p. 88 bottom left, p. 90 top, p. 90 bottom, p. 92 top left, p. 92 bottom left, p. 92 bottom right; O'Dell Manufacturing Company: p. 14 top right, p. 72; *The Orchid Digest:* p. 49 top; Riekes Crisa Corporation: p. 6 top, p. 6 bottom, p. 12, p. 13, p. 14 bottom left, p. 19, p. 20, p. 21 top, p. 21 bottom, p. 22 top, p. 22 bottom, p. 23, p. 24, p. 26, p. 29, p. 32 top, p. 32 bottom; Rohm and Haas Company: p. 7, p. 10, p. 14 top left; Sequoia Nurseries, p. 77 left; Fred A. Stewart, Inc.: p. 50 top; Terrestrial Terrariums: p. 25, p. 38, p. 43; Vaungarde, Inc.: p. 51 top.

Contents

1
The Miracle of the Terrarium

Almost two hundred years ago English gardeners began to bring ferns and flowering potted plants indoors from their conservatories and glasshouses and enclose them individually in bell jars and other glass containers. The benefits were obvious. Delicate leaves and pampered flowers enjoyed a relatively warm and moist atmosphere in these enclosures. However, it was not until around 1829 when Nathaniel Ward, an Englishman variously described as botanist, surgeon, and scientist — all of which he may well have been — discovered that a little soil and some plants sealed in a glass container could exist, indeed thrive, indefinitely, forming a perfect microcosm of nature. Actually, the discovery happened by accident. Dr. Ward enclosed a chrysalis with some garden soil in a jar. Since any healthy garden soil contains seeds and possibly other living plant matter, in time green growth appeared. What happened to the chrysalis we do not know, but Dr. Ward had the good sense to appreciate what was happening with the plants inside the jar and to document his findings in a scientific journal.

So it is that we honor Dr. Ward as the father of the Victorian Wardian case, which has, in the form of terrariums and bottle gardens, truly come of age. Those earlier gardeners had the idea, but they didn't write it down in the proper fashion. If we trace the development and early practical application of Dr. Ward's discovery, it is easily understood why the idea works so well for us today. Following that first sealed jar, he built large glass cases, which were used by early explorers to keep newly discovered plants alive during long sea voyages. It was not long before these practical cases were made up into the ornate glass enclosures for exotic plants which we associate with the Victorian drawing room. Keeping tropicals in those drafty, chill rooms was hopeless until the Wardian case came along.

Wardian cases soon became popular in drawing rooms in the more genteel American homes. Presumably this practice continued until central heating arrived. Just how those elegant under glass gardens evolved into the terrarium of today is not so easily traced. Conjecture has it that teachers, wishing to re-create Dr. Ward's discovery for students, began to refer to the glass jars and other containers as terrariums — *terra* meaning "earth" and *arium* meaning "home." It was probably one of those students who decided once again that

ABOVE: Peperomias and dwarf palm provide a woodland home for a pair of fine feathered figures in a carriage lantern hanging terrarium.

BELOW: Covered bubble bowl is planted with grape-ivy, hoya or wax plant, and a rooted tip cutting of crassula.

the time was right to try some small exotic plants in a glass enclosure and the old idea found a new life.

In the 1940s I remember as a small school child reading in gardening books about converting fish tanks into terrariums and removing the bottoms of five-gallon water jugs to make bell-jar coverings for temperamental plants. I had a lot of fun digging up seedlings from our Western Oklahoma ranch pasture land and watching them grow in the various terrariums I rigged up. In those days the prescribed method for removing the bottom from a glass jug was to score a line with a glass cutter where the break was desired, then tie a kerosene-soaked string in the scored line, set fire to the string, and immediately plunge the bottle in cold water. I never succeeded with this method, but today my own children seem to have mostly successes with the simple bottle-cutting kits which are sold everywhere.

By the late 1950s, when I first moved to New York, terrariums were being widely used as propagating boxes for rooting cuttings of such plants as African violets, gloxinias, and rex begonias. New or old, discarded fish tanks were the most popular choices, although I remember making one excellent propagating box simply by taping four pieces of glass together, setting them inside a slightly larger wooden seed flat and covering the top with a fifth piece of glass. In a north-facing window, as well as under fluorescent lights, this made a great place to grow miniature plants. I also remember tramping through the Connecticut woods property owned by a friend and scooping up a little of this and that and placing it in a five-gallon aquarium. This rather haphazard planting yielded a phenomenal array of mosses, ferns, violets, and a clump of bluets that bloomed for weeks in a north window of my New York City apartment.

By the early 1960s terrariums were beginning to be more decorative. One perfect,

OPPOSITE: Plexiglas acrylic sheeting is an excellent raw material for making your own terrarium. This decorative display includes a closed terrarium planting of ferns, podocarpus, Norfolk Island pine, and Trileaf Wonder (Syngonium) atop another cube enclosing a piece of sculpture. Pots of African violets on marble chips complete the setting.

A brandy snifter planting that was cultivated under fluorescent lights (a bright north window would also be fine).   *Plants include miniature caladium, miniature gloxinia, and three kinds of selaginella.*

flower-covered African violet was often seen planted in a large brandy snifter. The miniature gloxinia, *Sinningia pusilla,* was new on the scene and right away we realized that it needed constant warmth and high humidity. Some kind of terrarium was the answer. This era also brought bags and rolls of thin polyethylene plastic. Gardeners more intent on success with plants than esthetics found it a simple matter to enclose almost any container of plants in this wonderful new material. This was also the decade of awakening to the meaning of such words as environment, ecology, and pollution.

However awed, overwhelmed, or even angry those words made us feel, they brought into the 1970s an interest in gardening that is unprecedented in history. Ecological problems of this planet concern us all, yet few of us actually deal with them. It may sound foolish, but it is true that each time another person begins to grow plants at home, the world gets a little better. But growing plants at home is not always a successful venture. For some it is a real disappointment. Lack of experience and forgetting to water are only part of the problem. Modern houses and apartments, however well heated in winter and cooled in summer, tend to be as dry as the desert. We have hot, dry drafts more lethal to delicate plants than the chill of a Victorian parlor. And we travel frequently, for business or pleasure, leaving potted plants to certain neglect. A well-conceived, healthy terrarium is the best way to have thriving plants within the circumstances of today's lifestyle.

The farther we get from a farming society, and the higher up we live in sky-reaching apartments, the more we become strangers to nature. And there lies the most important benefit to be derived from growing miniature gardens in glass — or clear plastic — containers. It goes much farther than plunking a few little plants in a jug or plastic bubble. It is plants and people together, or more vitally, plants and you, the individual, living healthfully and relating to each other. The growing pleasure of a terrarium lies in creating a living, changing, interrelating microcosm of nature. Only certain kinds of plants go well together. It may remind you of the desert, of a woodland dell where you had a secret hid-

Instant terrarium: A rooting leaf of 'Cleopatra' begonia is given the moist environment it likes by simply covering it with a drinking glass.

ing place as a child, or of a Japanese landscape you may never have visited but whose peacefulness you felt. Within the confines of a glass or plastic container you hold in your hands all of these miracles. The range of possibilities and realizing them are what this book is about. Whether you talk to your plants or play music for them is of less importance than the time you spend nurturing growth, appreciating the curve of a leaf, the furl of a flower petal, and the smell of good moist earth.

The Miracle of the Terrarium   9

Watermelon-begonia (Peperomia), *pothos, strawberry-geranium* (Saxifraga), *dwarf palm, aluminum plant, and* Dracaena godseffiana *get along well together in a Plexiglas bubble bowl.*

2
Terrariums – Types, Planting, Maintaining

All you need to know to plant and to maintain a single but immensely satisfying terrarium could be written on a single page, yet the full scope of the subject easily merits an entire book. If you learn the basics, then you will be able to apply them to almost any situation, regardless of the container or plants available.

In the most general terms all terrariums may be classed as either open or closed. These two words are very important for they relate to the amount of natural light a terrarium planting can tolerate.

Open terrariums can tolerate some direct sunlight shining on them. However, if leaves are next to the walls of the terrarium, long periods of sun shining directly through the walls onto the leaves may burn them. An open terrarium is one with an opening equal to half or more of the container's dimensions. For example, a rectangular aquarium or straight-sided cylinder without any top is completely open. A brandy snifter without a cover is considered an open terrarium. A typical glass bubble bowl without a cover may be considered to be about half open.

Closed terrariums may be any of the containers suggested in the previous paragraph with the addition of a clear glass or plastic cover. All bottles and jugs, with or without a cork or plug, are closed containers insofar as the effect of direct sunlight on them is concerned. Closed terrariums are best positioned in strong natural light with little or no sun shining on them. They are ideal subjects for cultivating in fluorescent-light gardens. For brief periods of time, up to a week or two, terrariums cultivated in fluorescent-light gardens may be moved around the house for decorative purposes, but again, not where sun will shine directly on them.

What all this means is that if you want to grow sun-loving plants in a terrarium in natural light, then it will have to be open. This is fine if you have sufficient sunlight and if the plants you want to grow will thrive in the open air of your home. In such a terrarium, there will be slightly more moisture — humidity — in the air immediately surrounding the plants than elsewhere. If you want to grow terrarium plants that require high humidity, the container will have to be closed. This means that if you want to grow them in natural light, your selection will be limited to shade plants. To grow plants that need

some sun in a closed terrarium, a fluorescent-light setup for gardening is necessary.

In the Little Encyclopedia of Terrarium Plants, Chapter 4, you will find an additional discussion of the terms *open* and *closed* as they relate to the selection and culture of various plants.

Selecting a Terrarium Container

The marketplace today is filled with all kinds of terrariums — open and closed. Most of these are excellent. The only fault I find is that occasionally a terrarium only 6 or 8 inches in diameter will be offered with 5 or 6 plants that will soon if not immediately crowd each other to the point of poor health and poor looks.

Which brings up the point that almost any *clear* (not tinted) glass or plastic container may be used as a terrarium. It is merely a matter of fitting plants suitable to each other and to the size and shape of the container.

You do not necessarily have to buy a container in order to have a terrarium. Fruit jars, gallon-size pickle and mayonnaise jars (available for the asking from commercial kitchens), wine and water jugs, decanters and laboratory glassware all make fine terrariums. A 2-inch plastic cube, the top half clear, in which 35mm. color slides are stored, makes a perfect terrarium for a single plant of *Sinningia pusilla* or any other miniature gloxinia. Underwear, pantyhose, and stationery sometimes come in clear plastic containers which are sturdy enough to convert into terrariums.

Terrariums are not limited to table-top and shelf display. Some are ready-made to be hung from the ceiling or from a bracket mounted on the wall. Others are available in the form of tables or as spheres or egg shapes mounted on a pedestal.

LEFT: A hanging bubble bowl planted with dwarf palm, hoya, and young plants of echeveria. A miniature bridge provides a Japanese landscape effect. Use macrame skill to fashion a sling for hanging.

RIGHT: In this bubble bowl terrarium two ceramic butterflies adorn Dracaena sanderiana, variegated peperomia, aluminum plant, Philodendron sodiroi and partridge berry. Keep closed terrariums out of direct sun.

LEFT, ABOVE: Half-sphere wall-mounted terrarium made of Plexiglas. White marble chips set off plants, which include dark-leaved peperomia, ardisia, miniature African violet and small-leaved English ivy.

LEFT: Small bubble bowl has base filled with black charcoal chips. It holds spotted-leaved Dracaena godseffiana *and cutting of hypocyrta (goldfish plant).*

ABOVE: This six-sided terrarium has its own stand and a built-in light fixture to supplement natural light. Plants include fittonia, aluminum plant, Dracaena sanderiana, *and sansevieria.*

Red partridge berries, rattlesnake plantain (woodland orchid), sphagnum and kelley moss all thrive in this closed terrarium.

By using plate glass, Plexiglas, or Lucite and appropriate epoxy adhesives, it is possible to create your own terrariums as illustrated in some of the accompanying photographs. Thin redwood strips or leaded glass may be used to create elaborate fern and Wardian cases that hark right back to ornate Victorian times. Ob-viously, this business of terrarium gardening can take you almost anywhere — from the kindergarten simplicity of putting a cup of moist soil in a quart jar with a bean seed to the ultimate in sophisticated gardening and such crafts as glass cutting, designing in Plexiglas or Lucite, and wielding a soldering iron to

ABOVE: Materials often used in terrarium/bottle garden plantings: back row, l. to r.: white perlite, sphagnum peat moss, milled sphagnum moss. Front row, l. to r.: vermiculite, sand, packaged terrarium potting soil.

BELOW: To moisten dry planting soil, place desired quantity of soil in small plastic bag; pour in small amount of water; knead the soil-filled bag to distribute the moisture throughout the soil.

create works of art in leaded glass containers. Another craft possibility is the designing and knotting of macramé holders for hanging terrariums.

Terrarium Planting

When it comes to planting a terrarium, those two important words *open* and *closed* take on a slightly different meaning. Consider your terrarium *open* if you can get your hands, one or both, inside to do the planting and maintenance. Consider it *closed* if you cannot reach all the way inside with one hand.

Planting an open terrarium is of course much easier than one that is closed, so let's start at the beginning and work up to the more difficult. No special tools are needed to plant an open terrarium. Besides a selection of plants you will need:

1. Crushed gravel of ⅛-inch size
2. Crushed charcoal
3. Packaged potting soil

You will find both gravel and charcoal available wherever potted plants are sold, or obtain them by mail from terrarium specialists (see Chapter 10). General purpose potting soils are almost always too heavy in texture for terrarium plantings. Either purchase one labeled specifically for terrariums or alter general-purpose potting soil by mixing it with equal parts vermiculite or perlite (both sold in small bags wherever potted plants are available).

Before you add any ingredients to a terrarium first wash the container in warm water to which a little household detergent has been added. Rinse well in clean water, then dry completely. To begin planting, the basic procedure is to add:

1. A layer of gravel;
2. A layer of charcoal; and
3. A layer of potting soil.

How much of each you add depends on the size and depth of the container. Generally speaking the total depth of the three layers should add up to one-third the height of the

ABOVE: *Use warm, sudsy water to clean thoroughly all terrariums before planting. Rinse with clean water.*

BELOW: *Dry the container inside and out. Let it stand to air-dry completely before beginning planting.*

ABOVE: *Add the first layer of material. Here white marble chips are used.*

BELOW: *After plants are in place, florist's sheet moss is used to provide a carpet all around them.*

ABOVE: *Then add second layer. Charcoal chips are used here to help keep the soil fresh-smelling.*

BELOW: *When planting is finished, use soft-bristled brush to remove stray soil from leaves and inside walls.*

Curly-top terrarium. The white perlite surface contrasts with the small rocks and stones. Plants are peperomia, ardisia, miniature Gesneria cuneifolia (almost everblooming), and syngonium.

container. If the container is 9 inches tall you might add a ½-inch layer of gravel, a ½-inch layer of charcoal, and a 2-inch layer of potting soil for a total of 3 inches. Good gardeners like good cooks develop a sixth sense of what is right in any given situation; some are born with this but most of us develop it by experience.

As you add the layer of potting soil, keep in mind the kind of terrain you want in the finished planting. It can be level like the Texas prairie or gently rolling with hills and valleys. In a fairly large terrarium, chunks of soft pumice rock, in which you can hollow out planting pockets for selected plants, can be used if you want the effect of mountains; or put them into the holes of interestingly shaped, partially decayed wood or driftwood.

Next comes the placement of plants. I find it best generally to add the largest ones first. In some plantings these will represent trees and shrubs in a full scale landscape. In others the

A Japanese figurine gives an Oriental-garden feeling to this pinch-sided covered bowl terrarium. Lining the figure's way are podocarpus, peperomia, ardisia, and pilea.

largest, feature plant may be something like a flowering African violet. Remove each plant from the pot in which it has been growing. Using your fingers, gently work away some of the soil so that the roots are free to nestle into the terrarium soil.

After the larger plants are in place you can add the ground covers — little creepers and carpeters that help give a terrarium a finished appearance.

Next come the finishing touches, and herein lies a world of imagination. If you want the effect of a woodland dell, then you will probably add bits of lichen and mosses, perhaps a few twigs or chunks of weathered bark.

If you are working with cacti and other succulents to create a desertscape, sand is the obvious finishing touch (for the soil, see Chapter 5).

If you want an Oriental landscape in miniature, experiment with rounded, water-polished stones. You might also add an area of sand which can be raked, Japanese-fashion, with the tines of a fork.

One of the simplest ways to complete a terrarium is to carpet any bare soil with pieces of woods moss, florists' sheet moss (available from most local florists), or marble chips.

I have previously given short shrift to the use of animal and human figurines in terrarium plantings. But having seen them used tastefully by my fellow authors Virginie and George A. Elbert, Jack Kramer, and Charles Marden Fitch, I have changed my mind. In fact, as I have been writing my daughter Jeannene returned from vacation with a little keepsake bird fashioned of seashells and placed it immediately in her terrarium. I have to admit the effect is delightful. Now I think of what Jeannene and I might create using dollhouse furniture. Over a patch of green moss, for example, why not spread a tiny picnic cloth complete with doll dishes and a Lilliputian food basket?

This is a marvelous side benefit of terrarium gardening as a hobby. People of all ages enjoy it alone or together. Shopping for the plants is only the beginning. There's the fun of searching through antique and junk shops with an eye for discovering some great container for a

ABOVE: An open globe terrarium with ceramic partridges amid ardisias, pilea, and interesting twigs.

BELOW: Canister terrarium with miniature English ivy, selaginellas, and a rooted tip cutting of Christmas cactus.

ABOVE: Seedling of feathery fine Asparagus plumosus *grows in a bowl with tiny seashells accompanied by one larger shell for accent.*

BELOW: Crystal ball with plastic base forecasts a world of miniature gloxinia, podocarpus, fittonia, and selaginella.

terrarium or an interesting figurine, to mimic the human or animal scale. Collections of stones or seashells can provide the design of a terrarium in a unique display.

A body of water in your terrarium scheme can be simulated by clever placement of a small pocket mirror, or you can actually use a shallow container of water. Which brings me to another suggestion: From time to time insert a small vial of water in your terrarium and place in it some beautiful flower, perhaps picked from your garden indoors or outdoors, or salvaged from a bouquet you are about to throw away. Especially delightful in the spring are a few stems of lily-of-the-valley, wild sweet violets, forget-me-nots, or primroses.

As you shape the placement of plants, remember to check the appearance from the front as well as the top. If a container will be viewed from all sides, your design becomes more complicated than if it will be viewed primarily from only one side. Looking directly into the sides you actually can see the outer edges as a frame for the picture you create inside.

Consider also the appearance of the gravel, charcoal, and potting soil. The different textures and colors are usually attractive, but if you prefer a more subtle appearance, it is possible to work woods moss and florists' sheet moss, green side facing out, between the walls of the container and the various layers of the growing medium.

If you are planting in a tall container you may want to add more than the three layers of gravel, charcoal, and potting soil. You might alternate layers of gravel, sandstone pebbles, charcoal, and sand of various colors, finally topping them with potting soil. Pieces of nylon stocking cut slightly smaller than the dimensions of the container and placed on top of each layer will help keep the different layers unmixed over a long period of time.

OPPOSITE: Plantings in this covered brandy snifter include young sempervivums, maranta (prayer plant), rooted tip cuttings of Zebrina, dwarf palm, and a miniature gloxinia in bloom. Because of moisture, real-feathered bird will eventually deteriorate. Use only figurines of durable materials in your terrariums.

Variegated 'Glacier' English ivy, Dracaena godseffiana, *and podocarpus are handsomely set off by the sandpainting at the base of this candy jar canister terrarium.*

The most recent development in terrarium plantings has been the use of different colored sands to create the effect of a painted desert in the lower part of the container with plants above. Packets of many-colored sand are available wherever terrarium supplies are sold. I feel these sand paintings are more natural in the company of cacti and other desert succulents than with jungle foliage and flowering plants.

Basic Terrarium Maintenance

After all plants and finishing touches are in place, take a soft-bristled camel's-hair brush and remove bits of soil and moss from leaves and the walls of the container. Using a bulb baster from the kitchen, add only enough water to barely moisten the roots in place. Re-member, terrariums have no provision for drainage of excess water. Add a little water in the beginning. The next day poke your finger in the surface soil. It should feel nicely moist; not wet and muddy, not dusty and dry.

If your terrarium with a large opening has a cover, put this in place as soon as you have finished watering. If, after the cover is in place for a few days, the walls of the terrarium are completely clouded with condensed moisture so the plants are not clearly visible, remove the cover overnight; replace the following morning. If, after a few hours, the walls are again clouded with moisture, repeat the procedure. Continue this practice until the walls are mostly free of extensive condensation.

When to add water is one of the most difficult aspects of terrarium gardening. However, in containers with openings you can put your

A sandpainting of a mountainous landscape forms the base of this Plexiglas terrarium "house." Plantings include English ivy, pilea, pteris ferns, and selaginella.

hand through, deciding is somewhat easier. For plants in the *humusy moist* category (described in detail on page 34), the top inch of potting soil should feel barely moist before you add water. Plants in the *desert* category (see Chapter 5) should have water added if the soil an inch below the surface feels only faintly damp to your finger. The roots of cacti and other succulents are highly susceptible to rot if overwatered, especially immediately after transplanting.

The rest of terrarium maintenance is mostly routine garden work on a miniature scale. Clip and remove any dead leaves or spent flowers. Prune back any plant that is growing too large or rank in height or girth. If a plant dies, or is obviously too large for the container, replace it with another.

Is feeding necessary? Sometimes, but not al-

ways. After a terrarium planting has been growing for about three months, I usually add a little diluted fertilizer three or four times a year, mixing it at one-fourth the usual strength for potted house plants and adding it then as a part of the watering routine.

What about pests inside a terrarium? They're not likely to bother if you have examined and cleaned every plant carefully before placing it inside the terrarium. Even so, you may occasionally discover a slug or snail dining inside. Insects like mealybugs, red spider-mite, cyclamen mite, white fly, scale, and thrips (what a formidable lineup!) require a different tactic. Whatever you do, do not spray an aerosol of house-plant pesticide inside a terrarium; it will coat the walls with an oily film that is difficult to remove. One easy way to eradicate these insects is to cut off an inch-long

A shallow bowl planting with two kinds of hoya (wax plant), ardisia, watermelon-begonia peperomia, and a variegated-leaved peperomia. Tall ardisia is overgrown and should be removed to give remaining plants more room.

piece of a Shell No-Pest Strip and place it inside the terrarium. Fumes given off from the strip (Vapona is the chemical responsible) will kill the bugs without any further effort on your part. The other way is to mix a liquid house-plant pesticide in a small atomizer or plant mister; line the inside walls of the terrarium with paper toweling, then carefully spray the infested plants.

Complete overhaul of a terrarium is generally not needed for at least two years, if you are faithful about grooming and pruning the plants.

What about leaving your terrarium unattended? You are the best person to answer this, for you will discover how frequently each terrarium needs to be watered. Closed containers can be left unattended for weeks, if not months. If they are growing under fluorescent lights, it will be necessary to plug the unit into an automatic timer; 14 to 16 hours of light every day produce excellent results for most plants, although some gardeners reduce light to 12 hours in every 24 while they are absent for extended periods of time.

If you have an open terrarium growing in sunlight, especially if it is filled with plants other than cacti and succulents, they probably require fairly frequent applications of small quantities of water. If the time you will be away is longer than the usual lapse between waterings there are two things you can do: (1) Ask someone to come in and give your terrarium a drink of water — but leave written instructions about how much and how often, otherwise you may return to a bog garden; or (2) place a cover over your terrarium and move it out of direct sunlight.

3
Planting Bottle Gardens

Since you can't reach your hands into that small an opening to plant a bottle or other "closed" container, you will require some special tools. All of these tools you can improvise from materials found around most households:

1. Bulb baster from the kitchen for watering
2. A slender wooden dowel or bamboo plant stake at least 6 inches longer than the height of the bottle, or a planter tool (see page 30)
3. A length of wire coat hanger, bent with a small loop on one end to position plants and materials inside the bottle, with a handle by which to hold it bent on the other end (see shovel tool, page 30)
4. A second length of wire coat hanger with a bottle cork stuck onto one end (the cork must be slightly smaller than the bottle neck) to use as a soil tamper to firm roots in place, or a tamp tool (see page 30)
5. A second piece of wooden dowel with a single-edge razor blade attached to one end, or a pruning instrument (see page 31)
6. A funnel; or, instead, a piece of fairly stiff paper rolled into a funnel shape

In addition to these six bottle gardening tools, I sometimes have taped a demitasse spoon on the end of a long wooden dowel or bamboo stake to serve as a trowel. To remove particles of planting medium from the leaves you can tape a small camel's-hair brush to the same kind of dowel or stake. To remove dead leaves and flowers and growth you have cut with your pruning shears, a mechanic's pickup tool is a great help; you can purchase such tools at an automobile parts supply house or wherever terrarium supplies are sold. Long, slender, wooden terrarium tongs also make a worthwhile investment.

After you assemble your tools, plants, gravel, charcoal, potting soil, moss for ground cover, and any other finishing touches, clean the bottle. First rinse out with warm water to which a little household detergent has been added. Stubborn stains may require soaking for a time in household bleach. Of course, using an aerosol houseplant spray inside a laboratory flask that has a long, slender neck creates an impossible problem of cleaning, as implied in the previous chapter.

Once the bottle is clean, rinse it several times with clean water, then set

ABOVE: Start your bottle terrarium by pouring in the potting soil with the aid of a funnel.

BELOW: Position the plant and tamp soil around roots with long-handled tool or heavy-gauge wire.

Remove soil from the roots of the plant (in this case, a peperomia), and drop it through the bottle opening.

aside to dry in a warm place. If the inside walls are wet, every flying particle of planting medium will stick on them. When dry, you will have to use a funnel to add layers of gravel, charcoal, and potting soil. After you add each layer use a piece of dowel, bamboo stake, coat hanger with a loop, or stake with a demitasse spoon attached to shape the terrain.

Before you begin to place plants inside the bottle, set it on a piece of paper and, with a pencil, draw a line around it. Set the bottle aside and experiment with various arrangements of your plants inside the circle (or other shape) you have drawn. Once you have marked out an arrangement that is pleasing, proceed by inserting one plant at a time through the neck of the bottle and settling it in place as nearly as possible to the position it occupied on your paper pattern.

OPPOSITE: A wide mouth jar (opening is large enough for most hands to fit inside). Plants include syngonium, Gesneria cuneifolia, English ivy, selaginella, ardisia, and pteris ferns.

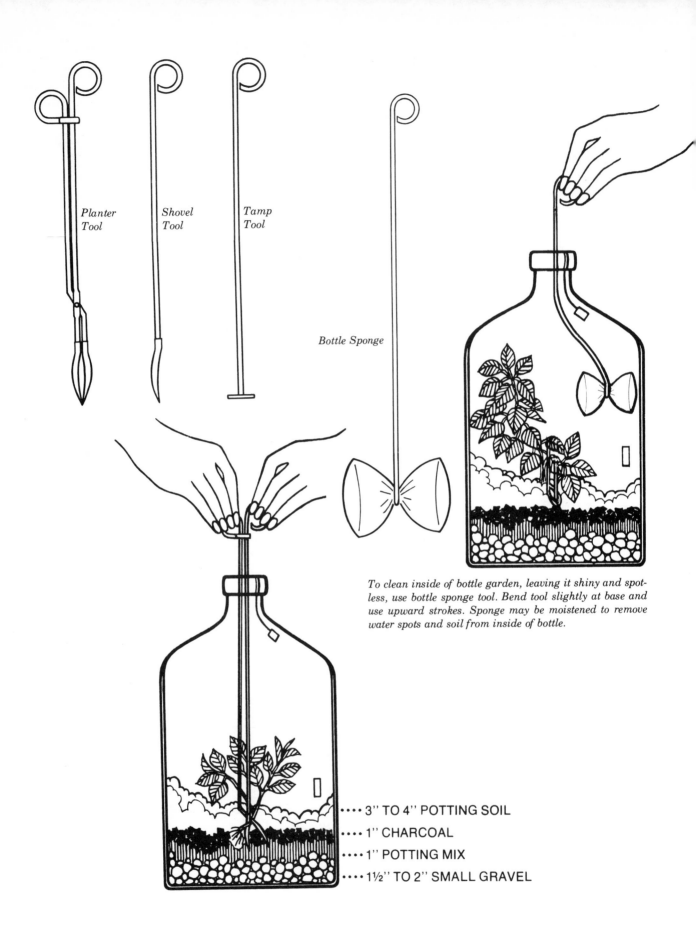

Planter Tool

Shovel Tool

Tamp Tool

Bottle Sponge

To clean inside of bottle garden, leaving it shiny and spotless, use bottle sponge tool. Bend tool slightly at base and use upward strokes. Sponge may be moistened to remove water spots and soil from inside of bottle.

···· 3'' TO 4'' POTTING SOIL

···· 1'' CHARCOAL

···· 1'' POTTING MIX

···· 1½'' TO 2'' SMALL GRAVEL

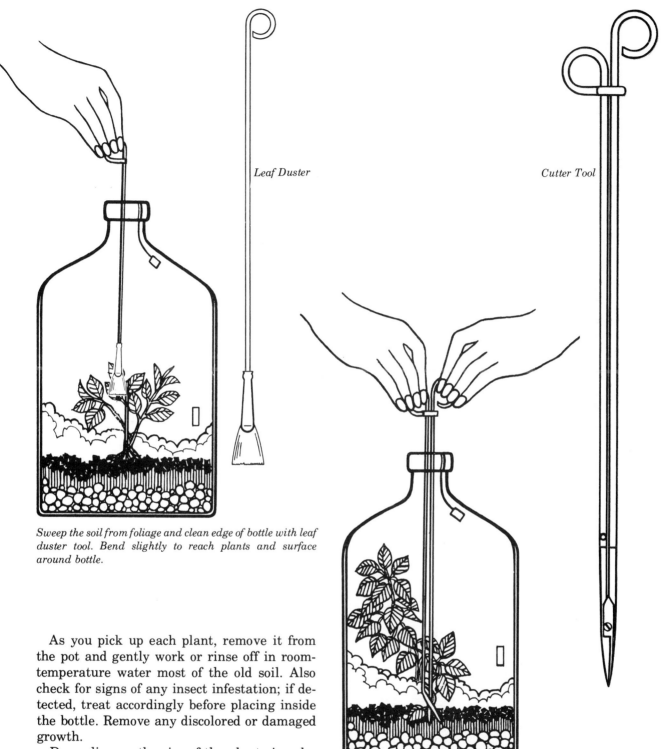

Leaf Duster

Cutter Tool

Sweep the soil from foliage and clean edge of bottle with leaf duster tool. Bend slightly to reach plants and surface around bottle.

As you pick up each plant, remove it from the pot and gently work or rinse off in room-temperature water most of the old soil. Also check for signs of any insect infestation; if detected, treat accordingly before placing inside the bottle. Remove any discolored or damaged growth.

Depending on the size of the plants in relation to the size of the bottle opening you may be able to lower them within the loop of your wire coat hanger tool, or you may have to simply coil the leaves gently around so that the plant alone slips through the neck and drops onto the

Place cutter in bottle garden and gently grip dead or unwanted leaves from plants; lift out of bottle with cutter. To remove plants that have grown too large, clip back with cutter tool at base of root (leave roots intact). Lift trimmings from bottle with tool.

soil surface. Once the plant is inside the bottle use one or more of your long-handled tools and position it and cover the roots with soil.

After all plants are in place you can proceed to add moss ground cover, pebbles, or any other finishing touches. Next, use the camel's-hair brush to clean foliage and flowers and the interior walls of any particles of earth. Finally, draw a little room-temperature water into the bulb baster and rinse down the walls and any leaves or flowers that may have stubborn particles of soil remaining on them. Be very careful about adding too much water to a bottle garden, however.

Maintenance thereafter is approximately the same for a closed terrarium as for one that is open.

An interesting alternative to placing plants inside a bottle is simply to plant a few seeds of one kind of plant, or perhaps several compatible kinds. In a very small bottle you might, for example, drop a few seeds of *Sinningia pusilla* or any other miniature gloxinia. Then you'll have the fun of watching for them to sprout, grow, and eventually reach flowering size. In a gallon to 5-gallon size bottle you might plant a few seeds of hybrid African violets, spores of miniature fern, or whatever small-growing plant appeals to you.

If all this sounds like a lot of trouble, may I assure you that there are terrariums which are practically carefree for months if not years. I have a 2-gallon bottle in my office bookcase that was planted five years ago with one rooted cutting of *Philodendron sodiroi*. Today it has nearly filled the space inside with silvery heart-shaped leaves, yet it receives only a half cup of water once every month or two. It has never been necessary to feed it or even to remove a dead leaf. I have seen similar bottle gardens filled with ferns or with selaginellas that exist beautifully with practically no care.

ABOVE LEFT: White and reddish brown stone chips accent a planting of two kinds of peperomia. Ardisia peeps out of the hand-cut hole.

LEFT: A large water bottle turned on its side with a hole cut in top (available commercially) for easy access. Plants have been planted at different levels for design interest. They include hoya (wax plant), peperomia, and ardisia.

4
Terrarium Plants

In each plant description that follows, you will find a set of cultural terms. To save space these are somewhat abbreviated. Here is the key:

Rooted Cutting: You may plant a rooted cutting in the terrarium, if so designated in the description. *Un*rooted cuttings of most plants placed in the constant warmth and moisture of a *closed* terrarium will promptly form roots and proceed into active growth.

Young Plant: One step beyond a rooted cutting; the sort of specimen shipped by many mail-order specialists, usually in a 2¼-inch pot. Also the kind of plant often found in the garden departments of dimestores, supermarkets, and florists.

Closed: This indicates a plant that tolerates — or needs — the relatively high humidity of a closed terrarium, which may be a container with a large opening that has a glass or plastic cover, or a bottle or jug with a small neck that may or may not have a cork or plug. Plants designated for a closed container that also require sun or half sun are best cultivated in fluorescent light.

Open: Such a plant either requires or will tolerate the open air of the indoor environment. A container is considered *open* if the opening is equal to half or more the dimensions of the container.

Warm: Translate to temperatures that would be comfortable for you, wearing normal at-home clothing. Specifically a range of 65° to 75° F.

Cool: A temperature range of approximately 50° to 60° F. in winter (while artificial heat is being used to warm the house or apartment).

Sunny: A situation that receives direct sunlight; east, south, and west windows generally qualify.

Half Sun: Very bright indirect light most of the day (for example, 5 feet back from a south-facing, sunny exposure), or a few hours direct sun early in the morning or late in the afternoon.

Note: Plants designated for *closed* and *half sun* require careful handling unless you cultivate them in a fluorescent-light garden. Be very careful about letting really hot midday sun shine directly on a closed terrarium or bottle garden. Plants that require some sun in combination with high humidity will generally adapt to a situation where daylight is constantly bright but without much sun shining directly on the leaves.

Fluorescent Light: Illumination for 12 to 16 hours out of every 24 in a fluorescent-light garden. Most terrarium plants do well in a range between 6 and 12 inches below the fluorescent tubes.

Woodsy Moist: This describes a humusy growing medium that is kept evenly moist at all times. Special terrarium planting mixes, sold as such in garden stores and plant shops, qualify as woodsy.

Desert: A sandy growing medium, indicated on the package as being formulated for cacti and other desert succulents. Maintain moisture in a range between nicely moist and nearly dry.

Osmunda and Fir-Bark: Some epiphytic orchids and bromeliads require osmunda or fir-bark as the growing medium. These are available mostly from growers who specialize in orchids and bromeliads.

As you make choices from these plants, keep in mind this basic, good rule of (green) thumb: You'll have best results if you combine plants with the same (or similar) cultural requirements in the same container. However, you can mix something that needs woodsy, moist soil with, for example, an epiphytic orchid or bromeliad that needs moist osmunda as the growing medium simply by raising this slightly above the soil level.

If you have a particular container in mind when you go shopping for terrarium plants, take along its dimensions and a ruler or tapemeasure. In this way you'll be prepared to purchase only plants of suitable size.

Sources for all of these plants are listed in Chapter 10; many of them may also be found locally.

Little Encyclopedia of Terrarium Plants

Abutilon: Flowering maple. *A. megapotamicum variegatum* has small variegated leaves on semitrailing stems, yellow flowers. Plant at the crest of a hill, mound, or rock in a large terrarium; stems need room to trail down in a cascade. Rooted cutting or young

ABOVE: Achimines 'Mexicana Blue.'

ABOVE: Ardisia. BELOW: Begonia 'Black Falcon.'

plant. Closed or open. Warm. Sunny to half sun. Fluorescent light. Woodsy moist.

Achimenes: Magic flower. A gesneriad, related to the African violet. Grows from a catkinlike scaly rhizome; plant in spring for summer and autumn flowers. Rest rhizomes in winter in darkness with moderate temperatures; keep nearly dry. During first two months of growth, pinch out growing tips frequently to encourage branching. For fairly large terrarium or case. Closed. Warm. Half sun. Fluorescent light. Woodsy moist.

Acorus: Miniature sweet flag. Select either *A. gramineus pusillus* or *A. g. variegatus.* Clumps of green or green-and-white leaves like 3-inch miniatures of common garden iris. Miniature. Closed. Cool to warm. Half sun to shade. Fluorescent light. Woodsy, very moist.

Actiniopteris: Fern. Miniature. Closed. Warm. Shade. Fluorescent light. Woodsy moist.

Adiantum: Maidenhair fern. Best for terrariums are the species that stay small naturally; for example, *A. bellum, A. diaphanum,* 'Ocean Spray,' and *A. reniforme.* However, a young plant of any maidenhair fern can be enjoyed for a time in cramped quarters and then transplanted elsewhere when it grows too large. Miniature or young plant. Closed. Cool to warm. Shade. Fluorescent light. Woodsy moist.

Aechmea: Bromeliad. Select naturally small-growing types, for example, *A. recurvata benrathii* and *A. tillandsioides,* or young plants of larger kinds. Closed. Warm. Half sun. Fluorescent light. Moist osmunda.

Aerides: Epiphytic orchids. Naturally small-growing kinds such as *A. crassifolium* and *A. japonicum* are best for terrariums. Closed. Warm. Half sun. Fluorescent light. Moist osmunda.

Aeschynanthus: Gesneriad. Lipstick Vine. Eventually becomes a large plant of many cascading stems; however, young rooted cuttings make fine terrarium plants. Excessive growth can be pruned off easily. Closed. Warm. Half sun. Fluorescent light. Woodsy moist.

Agalmyla: A little-known gesneriad, related to the African violet. Red flowers on creeping stems. Miniature. Closed. Warm. Half sun. Fluorescent light. Woodsy moist.

Aglaonema: Chinese evergreen. Superb foliage plants, unfortunately all too large for most terrariums. However, young plants may be enjoyed for some time. Foliage green, usually variegated with white, cream, yellow, or silver. Closed. Warm. Shade. Fluorescent light. Woodsy moist.

Allium: Chives. *A. schoenoprasum,* the chives used in cooking, are easily cultivated in a terrarium. The problem is that the plant tends to be stringy and weak unless it receives an abundance of light and fresh air. However, if you clip it back enough, the results are not all that bad, and besides you will have lots of fresh, tasty snippets to use in the kitchen. Start with seeds or a young, established plant. Open. Cool to warm. Sunny. Fluorescent light. Woodsy moist.

Allophyton: Mexican foxglove. Rosettes of quilted, dark green leaves with clusters of white, lavender, and purple foxglovelike flowers on slender 6-inch stems. Miniature. Closed. Warm. Half sun. Fluorescent light. Woodsy moist.

Alloplectus: Extraordinarily handsome — and large — foliage plants, related to the African violet. They require more warmth and humidity than can be provided in the open air of most homes, but young plants or rooted cuttings can be cultivated quite well in a large terrarium. Closed. Warm. Half sun. Fluorescent light. Woodsy moist.

Alternanthera: Dwarf Joseph's coat. Rooted cuttings or young plants. Shear or clip back regularly to maintain compact growth. Closed or open. Warm. Sunny. Fluorescent light. Woodsy moist.

Ananas: Pineapple. Miniature *A. nanus* is suitable for a fairly large terrarium. Closed. Warm. Sunny to half sun. Fluorescent light. Woodsy moist.

Anoectochilus: Dwarf jewel orchid. *A. sikkimensis* is excellent for terrariums. Closed. Warm. Half sun to shade. Fluorescent light. Woodsy moist.

Anthurium: Related to the philodendron. Species *A. clarinervum* and *A. crystallinum* have green heart-shaped leaves with silvery white veins. Showy in a fairly large terrarium. Closed. Warm. Half sun to shade. Fluorescent light. Woodsy moist.

ABOVE: Begonia weltonensis. BELOW: Begonia 'Iron Cross.'

BELOW: Miniature rex begonia.

Aphelandra: Zebra plant. Rooted tip cuttings are excellent in a terrarium. When an aphelandra begins to outgrow the space, simply chop it back and make new cuttings of appropriate size. Closed. Warm. Half sun. Fluorescent light. Woodsy moist to wet.

Araucaria: Norfolk Island Pine. Seedlings of *A. excelsa* grow slowly and may be enjoyed for up to two years — or even more — in a terrarium. Closed. Cool to warm. Half sun to shade. Fluorescent light. Woodsy moist.

Ardisia: Coralberry. Seedlings and rooted cuttings are popular for terrariums. Nipping out the growing tip will encourage branching. After a few years it will be necessary to root cuttings as older plants become fairly large, woody shrubs. Closed or open. Cool to warm. Half sun to shade. Fluorescent light. Woodsy moist.

Ardisiandra: A miniature relative of the primrose. Closed. Cool to warm. Half sun. Fluorescent light. Woodsy moist.

Ascocentrum: Orchid. *A. miniatum* is especially suited to a terrarium. Closed. Warm. Half sun to shade. Fluorescent light. Moist osmunda.

Asparagus: Young plants of *A. plumosus,* the kind of filmy fernlike leaves you see with a bouquet of roses, may be cultivated in a terrarium. Since this plant has a large and voracious root system, you will find it best to keep it confined in a pot, which you can conceal with rocks or a mound of soil. Closed or open. Warm. Half sun to shade. Fluorescent light. Woodsy moist.

Asplenium: Young plants of the bird's-nest fern (*A. nidus*) and the mother fern (*A. viviparum*) are outstanding for terrariums. Closed. Warm. Shade. Fluorescent light. Woodsy moist to wet.

Aucuba: Gold dust tree. Young, rooted tip cuttings of this plant do well for several months, if not more, in a fairly large terrarium. Green leaves dusted and flecked with golden yellow. Closed or open. Warm. Half sun to shade. Fluorescent light. Woodsy moist.

Begonia: Some of the most beautiful of all begonias grow best in terrariums where they can be surrounded constantly by warmth and high humidity. Some of the best from which to select include: *B. aridicaulis,* 'Baby Perfection,' *B. bartonea* (winter jewel), *B. boweri,* 'Bownigra,' 'Chantilly Lace,' 'China Doll,' 'Dawn,' 'Edith M,' *B. hirtella nana,* 'It,' *B. masoniana* (iron cross), 'Medora,' 'Persian Brocade,' *B. prismatocarpa* and *B. rex* cultivars 'Baby Rainbow,' 'Dew Drop,' and 'Silver Dawn.' The exquisite *B. imperialis* and its varieties are also excellent, either alone in a small container (for example, a 12-inch bubble bowl with lid) or in a fairly large terrarium with other plants. Closed. Warm. Half sun to shade. Fluorescent light. Woodsy moist.

Bertolonia: Soft-haired and quilted leaves in colors reminiscent of begonias. Mostly low-growing and miniature. Closed. Warm. Shade. Fluorescent light. Woodsy moist.

Billbergia: Bromeliad. Rooted cuttings or young plants may be small enough to enjoy for a time in a terrarium. Closed. Warm. Sunny to half sun. Fluorescent light. Woodsy moist.

Biophytum: Sensitive life plant. A miniature difficult to obtain except in seed form. Closed. Warm. Sunny to half sun. Fluorescent light. Woodsy moist.

Boea: A flowering, upright, but miniature, relative of the African violet. Difficult to grow except in a terrarium. Closed. Warm. Half sun to shade. Fluorescent light. Woodsy moist.

Bulbophyllum: Orchid. Study current listings of orchid specialists to find miniature species which will be included along with other "botanicals." Closed. Warm. Half sun. Fluorescent light. Moist osmunda.

Buxus: Boxwood. *B. microphylla japonica* is especially useful in fairly large terrariums or trough gardens where a small green shrub is needed. Open. Cool. Sunny. Fluorescent light. Woodsy moist.

Caladium: Miniature *C. humboldtii* (sometimes called *C. argyrites*) is a jewel for terrariums — but difficult to obtain. Closed. Warm. Sunny to half sun; may adapt to shade. Fluorescent light. Woodsy moist.

Calathea: Showy tropical foliage plants. Study growers' listings (see Appendix A) for kinds that grow smallest by nature. One of the best for terrariums is *C. micans.* Closed. Warm. Half sun to shade. Fluorescent light. Woodsy moist.

Callisia: Small creeper related to the wandering Jew. Closed or open. Warm. Half sun. Fluorescent light. Woodsy moist.

Callopsis: Like a miniature calla-lily, to which it is related. Closed. Warm. Half sun to shade. Fluorescent light. Woodsy moist.

Carex: Grassy, tufting plants. Closed. Warm. Half sun to shade. Fluorescent light. Woodsy moist to wet.

Carissa: Natal-plum. *C. grandiflora nana* and other dwarf or miniature forms are best for terrariums. Closed or open. Warm. Sunny to half sun. Fluorescent light. Woodsy moist.

Ceropegia: Rosary vine. Dangling vines that become creepers in a terrarium. Do not plant in a bottle as *Ceropegia* requires too much cutting back to keep it in control. Closed or open. Warm. Sunny to shade. Fluorescent light. Woodsy moist to desert.

Chaenostoma: Little Stars. Shrubby, low perennial with flowers in season. Shear or clip back to encourage compact growth. Warm. Open or closed. Sunny or fluorescent light. Woodsy moist to desert.

Chamaedorea: Dwarf palm. *C. elegans bella* is the Neanthe bella of florists. Seedlings are excellent as "trees" in a terrarium planting with tiny creepers like selaginella and miniature flowering plants like *Sinningia pusilla.* Since palms do not lend themselves to pruning back, replacement with a new seedling may be required in a year or two. Closed. Warm. Shade. Fluorescent light. Woodsy moist.

Chamaeranthemum: Ground-hugging creepers with attractively variegated foliage. Miniature to dwarf in size. Closed. Warm. Half sun to shade. Fluorescent light. Woodsy moist.

Chimaphila: Pipsissewa. Princess pine. Ground carpeters found in pine woods. They appear to be seedling evergreens. If you own or have free access to the woods and want to try collecting one or two *Chimaphilas for a* terrarium, fine, otherwise order from a specialist. Closed. Cool. Shade. Fluorescent light. Woodsy moist.

Chirita: A gesneriad, related to the African violet. *C. sinensis* is a showy foliage plant, excellent for terrarium culture. Closed. Warm. Half sun to shade. Fluorescent light. Woodsy moist.

Upright hexagonal with variegated chlorophytum (spider plant), artillery fern, variegated plectranthus, and pellionia.

Chlorophytum: Spider plant. *C. bichetti* is the only form suited to permanent residency in a terrarium. It forms clumps of grassy green leaves with pure white margins. A choice plant. Closed or open. Warm. Half sun to shade. Fluorescent light. Woodsy moist.

Cissus: Young plants of miniature kangaroo vine (*C. antarctica minima*), *C. discolor* (sometimes called the rex begonia vine because of the beautiful foliage coloration), and miniature grape-ivy *(C. striata)* are excellent for large terrariums. Closed. Warm. Half sun to shade. Fluorescent light. Woodsy moist.

Citrus: Seedlings sprouted from pits saved from any citrus fruit — oranges, lemons, limes, grapefruits — make excellent terrarium plants. With a little pruning you can keep them small for many years. Closed or open. Warm. Sunny to half sun. Fluorescent light. Woodsy moist.

Codonanthe: A gesneriad, related to the African violet. Trailing stems set with small hairy leaves and fragrant white flowers. An excellent terrarium plant, especially in fluorescent-light gardens. Start with a rooted cutting or young, established plant. Closed. Warm. Half sun. Fluorescent light. Woodsy moist.

Coelogyne: Study catalogs of orchid specialists for smallest forms of this genus; you'll find them usually in the listings of "botanicals." Closed. Warm. Half sun. Fluorescent light. Moist osmunda.

Coffea: Coffee plant. Dwarf forms of *C. arabica* make fine terrarium plants. The foliage is bright green with a glossy sheen, reminiscent of the gardenia. Seedlings, rooted cuttings, or young plants. Closed. Warm. Half sun to shade. Fluorescent light. Woodsy moist.

Coleus: Persian carpet. This foliage plant tends to outgrow a terrarium quickly. However, tip cuttings will root almost immediately wherever you plant them in a moist growing medium and humid atmosphere. Keep pinching back to cause branching. Start with seeds, tip cuttings, or young, established plants. Closed or open. Warm. Sunny to half sun. Fluorescent light. Woodsy moist.

Columnea: A gesneriad, related to the African violet. Catalogs of gesneriad specialists include long listings of columnea species and hybrids. Best for terrarium plantings are kinds that have an upright or semiupright habit. Use rooted cuttings or young plants. Some columneas tend to be nearly everblooming in a terrarium. Closed. Warm. Half sun. Fluorescent light. Woodsy moist.

Cordyline terminalis minima *'Baby Ti.'*

Cordyline: Seedlings or rooted cuttings of the Hawaiian ti plant *(C. terminalis)* or its miniature form *(C. t. minima* 'Baby Ti') are excellent for terrariums. Closed. Warm. Half sun to shade. Fluorescent light. Woodsy moist.

Crossandra: Nearly everblooming with salmon-orange flowers and shiny, dark green foliage like a gardenia. Prune back as necessary to maintain desired size. Start with a seedling, a rooted cutting, or young plant. Closed. Warm. Half sun. Fluorescent light. Woodsy moist.

Cryptanthus: Earth stars. Of all the bromeliads, this genus currently offers the most material for terrarium plantings. They are also well distributed and not at all difficult

ABOVE: Crossandra. BELOW: Ctenanthe oppenheimiana tricolor.

BELOW: Dizygotheca.

to locate in local plant shops; easily obtainable by mail also. Closed or open. Warm. Half sun to shade. Fluorescent light. Woodsy moist to desert.

Ctenanthe: Showy tropical foliage plants. Only young specimens are suited to fairly large terrarium plantings. Closed. Warm. Half sun to shade. Fluorescent light. Woodsy moist.

Cuphea: Delicate appearing woody shrublet with narrow leaves and flowers of pink almost nonstop. Clippings made to maintain proper size and shape may be used for making miniature table flower arrangements. Start with rooted cuttings or a young, established plant. Closed or open. Warm. Sunny to half sun. Fluorescent light. Woodsy moist.

Cyanotis: Teddy-bear plant and pussy ears. Related to the wandering Jew. Succulent creepers. Start with rooted cuttings or young plants. Open. Warm. Sunny. Fluorescent light. Desert.

Cyclamen: Baby cyclamen, *C. neapolitanum,* is suited to a fairly large terrarium or trough garden in coolness only. Closed or open. Cool. Half sun. Fluorescent light. Woodsy moist.

Cymbalaria: Kenilworth-ivy. This creeping ground cover tends to take over a terrarium planting. However, if you keep it clipped and in its place, both the leaves and flowers are attractive. Start with a rooted cutting or young plant. Closed or open. Cool. Half sun. Fluorescent light. Woodsy moist.

Daphne: Small evergreen shrubs with intensely fragrant flowers. Young plants may be used in trough gardens or terrariums. Open. Cool. Half sun. Fluorescent light. Woodsy moist.

Davallia: Rabbit's-foot fern. Species *D. bullata* and *D. pentaphylla* are perhaps best in a terrarium, although a young (small), established plant of almost any species can be enjoyed for a time in a limited space. Closed. Warm. Half sun to shade. Fluorescent light. Woodsy moist.

Dieffenbachia: Dumb cane. This giant of the jungle is sometimes included in commercially planted terrariums and bottle gardens. This is always a mistake for the dieffenbachia has a large, hungry root system and it will almost immediately outgrow all but the largest of terrarium containers. If you receive a terrarium that includes a dieffenbachia, transplant it as soon as possible to a flower pot and replace it with something more suitable.

Diosma: Breath-of-heaven. Small shrub with pine-scented needles. Start with rooted cutting or young, established plant. Clip as necessary to maintain desired size and shape. Closed or open. Cool to warm. Sunny. Fluorescent light. Woodsy on the dry side.

Dizygotheca: False aralia. Seedlings of this plant, sometimes called false aralia or "the one that looks like marijuana," do well in terrariums for a year or two if not more. In combination with miniature creepers and little flowering plants (miniature African violets and gloxinias, for example), it will give the appearance of a palm tree. Closed or open. Warm. Half sun to shade. Fluorescent light. Woodsy moist.

Dracaena: Seedlings and rooted cuttings of many different kinds of dracaenas are widely distributed. Some of them make excellent terrarium plants for a year or two until they outgrow the space. Favorites include *D. godseffiana* (perhaps best of all as a permanent terrarium resident), *D. goldieana* while young (this particular species is difficult to find), and *D. sanderiana* (the striped leaf, bamboolike plant almost always included in commercially planted dish gardens). Closed or open. Warm. Half sun to shade. Fluorescent light. Woodsy moist.

Epigaea: Trailing arbutus. Young plants purchased from a wildflower specialist may be used in terrariums and trough gardens. Closed or open. Cool. Half sun to shade. Fluorescent light. Woodsy moist.

Episcia: Flame violet. A gesneriad, related to the African violet. Beautiful foliage varying from quilted, plain, bright green to all kinds of variegations — white, cream, pink, rose, bronze, and silvery. Flowers may be white, rose, yellow, scarlet, or lavender blue. Seedlings, rooted cuttings, or young plants. Closed. Warm. Half sun to shade. Fluorescent light. Woodsy moist.

Eranthemum: Blue sage. The species *E. nervosum* has bright blue flowers above dark green leaves. Seldom seen but very worthwhile. Start with a young plant which you will probably have to obtain by mail from a

ABOVE: Dracaena godseffiana *'Florida Beauty.'*

ABOVE: Dracaena sanderiana. *BELOW: Episcia hybrid.*

ABOVE: Episcia 'Harlequin.' BELOW: Episcia 'Pink Brocade.'

BELOW: Episcia dianthiflora.

specialist. Closed. Warm. Half sun. Fluorescent light. Woodsy moist.

Erythrodes: Jewel orchid. Exquisite foliage plants with small flowers in season. Available by mail from orchid specialists. Closed. Warm. Shade. Fluorescent light. Moist mixture of osmunda and unmilled sphagnum moss.

Euonymus: This common garden shrub is surprisingly useful in terrarium plantings, especially *E. japonicus microphyllus* and its variegated form. Closed or open. Cool to warm. Half sun to shade. Fluorescent light. Woodsy moist.

Exacum: Start these plants from seeds, which may be sown directly on the surface of moist soil in a terrarium. They bloom while quite young, especially well in a fluorescent-light garden. You'll have to constantly clip and remove dead flowers, but as new starry lavender-blue ones open, you will decide the upkeep is worthwhile. Closed or open. Warm. Half sun to shade. Fluorescent light. Woodsy moist.

Festuca: Blue fescue. Fine-textured blue-green leaves in clumps. Start with seeds or young plants. Open. Warm. Sunny. Fluorescent light. Woodsy moist to desert.

Ficus: Creeping fig. *F. pumila* and its smaller version, *F. p. minima,* make excellent carpeters for terrariums of all kinds. Start with rooted cuttings or young plants. Closed. Warm. Half sun to shade. Fluorescent light. Woodsy moist.

Fittonia: More or less ground-hugging foliage plants, green with white veins or green with rosy pink. Start with rooted cuttings or young plants. Closed. Warm. Half sun to shade. Fluorescent light. Woodsy moist.

Gesneria: This gesneriad, and African violet relative, is perhaps the best of all everblooming plants to grow in a terrarium. Kinds include *G. cuneifolia,* 'El Yunque,' 'Quebradillas,' 'Lemon Drop,' and the hybrid *G. pedicellaris* x *citrina.* Start with seeds, rooted cuttings, or young, established plants (available from gesneriad specialists). Keep dead flowers clipped off and removed from the terrarium. Closed. Warm. Half sun to shade. Fluorescent light. Woodsy moist.

Hexagonal terrarium with one panel removed for visibility in the photograph—and to facilitate planting and routine maintenance. Plants include fittonia, artillery fern, Victo- *rian table ferns (Pteris), miniature English ivy, and one rooted cutting of jade plant.*

Goodyera: Rattlesnake Plantain. A dwarf terrestrial orchid. Start with a young, established plant. Beautiful foliage for a terrarium. Closed. Cool to warm. Shade. Fluorescent light. Woodsy moist.

Guzmania: Bromeliad. Young plants of almost any species may be enjoyed for a time in a fairly roomy terrarium. Among the best is naturally small *G. lingulata minor flammea striata.* Closed. Warm. Half sun. Fluorescent light. Woodsy moist.

Hedera: English ivy. Small-leaved varieties are great to plant in all kinds of terrariums. Start with rooted cuttings or young plants. Miniatures tend to be upright, little bushes; others will trail or climb, depending on how you train them. Closed or open. Cool to warm. Half sun to shade. Fluorescent light. Woodsy moist.

Helxine: Baby's-tears. This little ground carpeter grows with abandon in terrariums — almost too well. Start with cuttings or young

This domed environment—called Terra-pet by the manufacturer—contains a ceramic turtle amid small-leaved English ivy, Helxine *(baby's-tears), pilea, moss, and a young fern.*

plants. Closed or open. Cool to warm. If open, best situated in half sun. If closed, best cultivated in a fluorescent-light garden. (Lack of sufficient light causes helxine to grow weak, stringy, and unattractive; in ample light it forms a dense mat on the surface of the ground.) Woodsy moist.

Hemigraphis: Red or flame ivy. The sort of foliage plant mostly overlooked in greenhouses and nurseries, but in the right terrarium setting it can be a beauty. Leaves metallic green with rosy or burgundy suffusion. Start with rooted cutting or established, young plant. Keep clipping back to encourage compact growth. Closed or open. Warm. Half sun to shade. Fluorescent light. Woodsy moist.

Hoya: Wax plant. Rooted cuttings and young plants of any *Hoya* may be used in terrarium plantings. Closed or open. Warm. Sunny to shade. Fluorescent light. Soil may be in a range from woodsy moist to dry (desert).

Hypocyrta: Gesneriad, related to the African violet. Study listings of gesneriad specialists and order only named hybrids such as 'Rio,' 'Mardi Gras,' and 'Tropicana.' Start with rooted cuttings or young, established plants. Closed. Warm. Half sun. Fluorescent light. Woodsy moist.

Hypoestes: Pink polka dot. Freckle Face. Olive-green leaves with pink spots and splashes. Start with a rooted tip cutting. Keep nipping and snipping or it will quickly outgrow the terrarium. Closed or open. Warm. Half sun. Fluorescent light. Woodsy moist.

Impatiens: Sultana. Any of the tender perennial *Impatiens* may be cultivated for a time as terrarium plants. The annual garden balsam is not suited to indoor culture. Of special note are the newer *Impatiens* from New Guinea which have highly colored foliage as well as flowers. Start with seeds, rooted cuttings, or young plants. Keep pruned back as necessary to maintain desired size. Closed or open. Warm. Sunny to half sun. Fluorescent light. Woodsy moist.

Iresine: Bloodleaf. Rosy red and reddish-purple leaves. Start with a young, rooted tip cutting. Tends to grow rampantly in a humid terrarium, but attractive if kept pruned. Also drops old leaves on the soil surface, so you'll have to do some raking. Closed or open. Warm. Sunny to half sun. Fluorescent light. Woodsy moist.

Jacobinia: In window gardens, greenhouses, and outdoors, this plant tends to be a gangly half shrub. Tip cuttings rooted in a terrarium often flower splendidly. When growth exceeds available space, remove and plant in a flower pot in the open; replace with a healthy tip cutting. Closed or open. Warm. Half sun. Fluorescent light. Woodsy moist to slightly dry.

Jasminum: Jasmine. *J. sambac* variety 'Maid of Orleans' makes an interesting trailer with fragrant white flowers for a fairly large terrarium. Start with a rooted cutting or young, established plant. Closed. Warm. Half sun. Fluorescent light. Woodsy moist.

Koellikeria: Small-growing member of the gesneriad family; culture is similar to that of the related *Achimenes* in that this plant also grows from a scaly rhizome. Closed. Warm. Half sun to shade. Fluorescent light. Woodsy moist.

Kohleria: This member of the gesneriad family grows from a scaly rhizome, as does the related *Achimenes*. Smaller growing *K. amabilis* and *K. lindeniana* have beautiful foliage as well as flowers in season. Tip cuttings of all

ABOVE: *Variegated* Euonymus japonicus microphyllus.

ABOVE: Ficus pumila. BELOW: Fittonia.

ABOVE: English ivy 'Glacier' (Hedera).

ABOVE: Ludisia *(jewel orchid). BELOW: Maranta.*

root fairly easily inside a terrarium, which means if the old plant grows too large, you simply remove it and replace with healthy cuttings. Closed. Warm. Half sun. Fluorescent light. Woodsy moist.

Lagerstroemia: Crape-myrtle. The dwarf crape-myrtlette introduced recently by the George W. Park Seed Company makes an excellent terrarium plant. Start with seeds or a young plant. Closed or open. Warm. Sunny to half sun. Fluorescent light. Woodsy moist.

Lobularia: Sweet-alyssum. This common garden annual is sometimes useful in a trough or tray garden, especially the double-flowered *L. maritima florepleno.* Start with seeds or young plants. Open. Cool. Sunny. Fluorescent light. Woodsy moist.

Lockhartia: Study catalogs of orchid specialists to find this attractive foliage and flowering plant for a terrarium. Start only with a flowering-size, established plant. Closed. Warm. Half sun to shade. Fluorescent light. Moist osmunda.

Ludisia: Jewel orchid. Sometimes listed by the name *Haemaria discolor dawsoniana.* Exquisite foliage is bronzy green with vivid pink veins. Obtain young plant from an orchid specialist. Closed. Warm. Shade. Fluorescent light. Woodsy moist.

Lycopodium: Club moss. Unusual green carpeters found on northern forest floors. Neither true mosses nor ferns, but sometimes confused with both. If you have your own woods and an abundance of club moss, try transplanting some to a terrarium. Otherwise, buy a young, established plant from a wildflower specialist. Closed. Cool. Shade. Fluorescent light. Woodsy moist.

Majorana: Sweet marjoram. Fragrant gray-green leaves on low, bushy plants. Start from seeds or purchase a young, established plant. Cut back as necessary to maintain desired size and shape; use clippings for seasoning. Open. Cool or warm. Sunny. Fluorescent light. Woodsy moist.

Malpighia: Miniature holly. *M. coccigera* forms a little twiggy shrub covered with miniature hollylike leaves. In season there are pink flowers. Start with a young plant. Prune it to shape as necessary. Closed or open. Warm. Sunny. Fluorescent light. Woodsy moist.

Neoregelia carolinae 'Tricolor.'

Maranta: Prayer plant. Tropical foliage, beautifully colored and patterned that folds up at night. In high humidity and insufficient light, marantas tend to grow too rangy for a small terrarium. Start with healthy, young, established plants. With age, older leaves naturally turn brown, curl up, and die. Clip them off and remove from the terrarium to avoid problems of disease. Closed. Warm. Half sun to shade. Fluorescent light. Woodsy moist.

Mimosa: Sensitive plant. *M. pudica* folds up its leaves at the slightest touch. Start from seeds. Remove from terrarium when the plant ceases to be attractive. Closed or open. Warm. Sunny to half sun. Fluorescent light. Woodsy moist.

Mitchella: Partridge-berry. Evergreen creeper often found growing wild in northeastern woodlands. Obtain established plants from a wildflower specialist. Closed. Cool. Half sun to shade. Fluorescent light. Woodsy moist.

Myrtus: Myrtle. *M. communis microphylla,* the dwarf myrtle, is especially suited to terrarium plantings. It can be clipped into miniature topiary shapes. Start with rooted cuttings or young, established plants. Closed or open. Cool to warm. Sunny to half sun. Fluorescent light. Woodsy moist.

Nautilocalyx: Primarily foliage plants of the gesneriad family, and related to the African violet. Start with small rooted cuttings; pinch back to encourage branching. When plant outgrows space, remove and start over with a cutting. Closed. Warm. Half sun to shade. Fluorescent light. Woodsy moist.

Neoregelia: Bromeliad. Almost any young neoregelia may be enjoyed for a time in a terrarium planting. In time it will outgrow the

A terrarium—called Terra-dome by the manufacturer—that provides perfect growing conditions for baby spider plant, syngonium (trileaf wonder), a very young Boston fern (Nephrolepis), selaginella, and miniature rex begonia.

space and you will have to replace it with something else. Closed. Warm. Half sun. Fluorescent light. Woodsy moist.

Nephrolepis: Boston fern. Young plants may be enjoyed for several months, if not a year or more, in a terrarium. Best suited for long-range, small-space culture are the more delicate kinds such as *Whitmanii* and *Norwoodii.* Start with small, young, established plants. Closed. Warm. Half sun to shade. Fluorescent light. Woodsy moist.

Nertera: Coral bead plant. Ground carpeting creeper covered in season by orange-red berries. Start from seeds. Closed. Cool. Half sun. Fluorescent light. Woodsy moist to wet.

Ocimum: Sweet basil. Sow a few seeds of either the green or purple leaf type. Or purchase young, established plants. Constantly pinch and clip to encourage bushy, compact growth; use what you cut off for seasoning. Open. Warm. Sunny. Fluorescent light. Woodsy moist.

Oncidium: Check listings of orchid specialists for miniature *Oncidiums.* Like many epiphytes, ideally they need an atmosphere of fresh, very moist air, but more and more growers are reporting success with miniature *Oncidiums* in terrarium conditions. Closed or open (with high humidity). Warm. Half sun. Fluorescent light. Moist to dry osmunda.

Ornithocephalus: Orchid. Species fairly easily obtainable from specialists grow only 1 to 3 inches tall. Ideal for terrarium culture. Invest only in established plants. Closed. Warm. Half sun. Fluorescent light. Moist osmunda or fir-bark.

Osmanthus: Sweet-olive. A young, established plant of *O. fragrans* makes an unusual tall shrub or treelike addition to a fairly large terrarium. In the right light it will be nearly everblooming, each small creamy-white flower intensely fragrant. Closed or open. Cool to warm. Half sun. Fluorescent light. Woodsy moist.

Oxalis: Fire fern. *O. hedysaroides rubra* makes a beautiful foliage plant in a terrarium. If it outgrows the space, prune excess growth. Start with a rooted cutting or young, established plant. Closed or open. Warm. Sunny to half sun. Fluorescent light. Woodsy moist. Ground-carpeting *O. martiana aureo-reticulata*

Oncidium macranthum, *an orchid.*

Oxalis hedysaroides rubra *(fire fern).*

ABOVE: *Assorted Paphiopedilums (ladyslipper orchids)*.

ABOVE: Peperomia *rubella*. BELOW: Peperomia *'Silver Ripples.'*

has typical four-leaf clover leaves, remarkably veined in bright yellow. Best suited to fluorescent-light culture. This oxalis increases by bulblets and spreads quickly in a terrarium. Closed or open. Warm. Sunny to half sun. Fluorescent light preferable. Woodsy moist.

Paphiopedilum: Ladyslipper orchid. Check listings of orchid specialists for low-growing *Paphiopedilums.* Buy established, flowering-size plants. Closed. Warm. Shade. Fluorescent light. Woodsy moist or moist osmunda.

Pelargonium: Geranium. Varieties of miniature geranium are the right size for a terrarium but almost impossible to grow well in the average house because winter temperatures are too high, especially inside a terrarium. Keep yellowing and dead leaves and flowers removed. Start with young, established plants or rooted cuttings. Open. Cool. Sunny. Fluorescent light. Woodsy moist to nearly dry.

Pellaea: Small-growing ferns. Start with young, established plants. Closed. Cool to warm. Shade. Fluorescent light. Woodsy moist.

Pellionia: Ground-carpeting creepers with handsomely variegated foliage. Start with rooted cuttings or young, established plants. Closed. Warm. Half sun to shade. Fluorescent light. Woodsy moist.

Peperomia: Dozens of foliage plants for terrarium plantings. Like begonias, they tend to be touchy about over- and under-watering. They usually do well in soil that varies between nicely moist and just slightly dry. Start with rooted cuttings or young, established plants. Closed or open. Warm. Half sun. Fluorescent light. Woodsy moist to slightly dry.

Petrocosmea: Little-known gesneriad, a relative of the African violet. White and cream-colored flowers set amidst the softly furred leaves. Start with a young, established plant. Closed. Warm. Half sun to shade. Fluorescent light. Woodsy moist.

Petroselinum: Parsley. Buy started plants or sow a few seeds. Open. Cool to warm. Sunny. Fluorescent light. Woodsy moist.

Phalaenopsis: Moth Orchid. Dwarf species and new dwarf hybrids are outstanding for terrarium culture, especially in a fluorescent-light garden. Invest only in established plants.

Closed. Warm. Shade. Fluorescent light. Moist osmunda or fir-bark.

Philodendron: In a small terrarium, *P. sodiroi* makes an excellent plant. It has silvery green, heart-shaped leaves and can be kept small almost indefinitely. In a larger container you can plant almost any small-leaved, trailing philodendron or enjoy one of the rarer climbing sorts by providing a tree-fern bark totem on which it can climb. Start with rooted cuttings or young, established plants. Closed. Warm. Half sun to shade. Fluorescent light. Woodsy moist.

Phinaea: A gesneriad, related to the African violet. Miniature with furry grayish leaves and white flowers. Start with a young, established plant. Closed. Warm. Half sun. Fluorescent light. Woodsy moist.

Pilea: Artillery fern. Aluminum plant. Panamiga. Creeping Charlie. English Baby's-tears. All of these popular names represent different species of *Pilea,* a very useful terrarium plant. Also to consider are the newer varieties, 'Black Magic,' 'Moon Valley,' and 'Silver Tree.' Start with rooted cuttings or young, established plants. Nip back growing tips frequently to encourage compact growth. From time to time you may find it necessary to prune more severely to keep growth within space limitations. Closed or open. Warm. Half sun to shade. Fluorescent light. Woodsy moist.

Platycerium: Staghorn fern. Young plants of this fern grow beautifully in large terrariums. Remove when they begin to crowd. Closed. Warm. Half sun to shade. Fluorescent light. Woodsy, moist osmunda.

Plectranthus: Swedish ivy. This plant tends to be rampant in a terrarium, yet nothing is so easy to obtain and to grow. Be prepared to do a lot of pruning and pinching to maintain compact growth of desired size. Start with cuttings, rooted or unrooted. Closed or open. Warm. Sunny. Fluorescent light. Woodsy moist.

Pleurothallis: Orchid. Select from true miniature species, listed in catalogs of specialists. Start with established plants. Closed. Warm. Shade. Fluorescent light. Moist osmunda or fir-bark.

Podocarpus: Young, rooted cuttings of this popular outdoor hedge plant and tree are excel-

ABOVE: *Jumbo terrarium with its own pedestal. Plants are* piggyback *(Tolmiea),* dwarf palm, aluminum plant, Philodendron sodiroi, *and silver-leaved Chinese evergreen (*Aglaonema*).*

BELOW: *Pellionia.*

Pilea microphylla, *the artillery fern.*

lent for terrariums. Closed or open. Cool to warm. Sunny to half sun. Fluorescent light. Woodsy moist.

Polypodium: Fern. Young plants of many species may be cultivated in terrarium gardens. Naturally small kinds like *P. lycopodioides* and *P. piloselloides* may be kept indefinitely in a terrarium. Closed. Warm. Half sun to shade. Fluorescent light. Woodsy moist.

Polyscias: Aralia. Rooted cuttings can be kept to terrarium size for months if not years by pruning now and then. Unusual crinkled, parsleylike foliage and gnarled, corky gray bark. Closed or open. Warm. Half sun to shade. Fluorescent light. Woodsy moist.

Polystichum: Various species of this fern may be enjoyed in a terrarium while they are young, but the best of all is a miniature, *P. tsus-simense,* which is a truly great fern. Start with a young, established plant. Closed. Warm. Shade. Fluorescent light. Woodsy moist.

Pteris: Victorian table fern. These are avail-

Podocarpus.

Pilea 'Moon Valley.'

Polystichum tsus-simense *and* Davallia *ferns.*

ABOVE: *Silver-and-green* Pteris *fern.* BELOW: *Plain green* Pteris *fern.*

BELOW: *Miniature African violet* (Saintpaulia) *'Pixie Blue.'*

able in almost countless forms. As young plants, all are useful in terrariums. Closed. Warm. Shade. Fluorescent light. Woodsy moist.

Punica: Pomegranate. *P. granatum nana*, a dwarf version, is fun to cultivate in a terrarium as a young plant. Prune as necessary to maintain desired shape and size. Beautiful flowers in season. Closed or open. Warm. Sunny. Fluorescent light. Woodsy moist.

Pyrola: Shinleaf. Beautiful green leaves grow in low rosettes. The flowers are tiny waxy bells, in season. If you have your spot of woodland, you may be able to find a spare *Pyrola* to transplant, otherwise purchase an established plant from a wildflower specialist. Closed or open. Cool. Half sun to shade. Fluorescent light. Woodsy moist.

Ramonda: A gesneriad, related to the African violet, but nearly cold-hardy in up-North gardens. Under the right conditions, it makes a fine terrarium subject. Start with seeds or a young, established plant. Closed or open. Cool. Half sun to shade. Fluorescent light. Woodsy moist to on the dry side.

Rechsteineria: A gesneriad, and related to the African violet. Tuberous-rooted, like the gloxinia (known botanically as *Sinningia*), which is also related. Rechsteinerias make fine plants for a large terrarium where the constantly warm, moist atmosphere will help flowers develop properly. Closed. Warm. Half sun to shade. Fluorescent light. Woodsy moist.

Rhipsalidopsis: A jungle cactus that resembles Thanksgiving and Christmas cactus. Start with a rooted cutting or young, established plant. Closed or open. Warm. Half sun. Fluorescent light. Moist fir-bark.

Rosa: Miniature rose. Start with a young, established plant. Prune back as necessary to maintain proper size. Best for a fairly large terrarium. Open. Cool to warm. Sunny. Fluorescent light. Woodsy moist.

Rosmarinus: Rosemary. The herbalists' *R. officinalis* makes an excellent terrarium plant. Start with a rooted cutting or young established plant. Save for seasoning the parts you clip back to maintain desired size and shape. Closed or open. Cool to warm. Sunny to half sun. Fluorescent light. Woodsy moist.

ABOVE: Saxifraga stolonifera *(strawberry-begonia).*

Ruellia: Tropical foliage and flowering plants. Start with rooted tip cuttings or compact, young, established plants. Closed. Warm. Half sun. Fluorescent light. Woodsy moist.

Saintpaulia: African violet. Miniature varieties make excellent flowering terrarium plants. In slightly larger quarters almost any African violet can be cultivated for a year or two. The species are also interesting for terrarium plantings. Start with seeds, rooted cuttings, or young, established plants. Closed or open. Warm. Half sun to shade. Fluorescent light. Woodsy moist.

Sansevieria: Common snake plant and the bird's-nest types may not be of much interest to you, but study listings in catalogs of specialists (see Appendix A) for unusual species. Mostly they are fairly large growing and more suited to dish or bowl gardens than to confinement in a terrarium. Start with young, established plants. Open. Warm. Sunny to shade. Fluorescent light (for suitably low-growing types). Woodsy moist to dry.

Saxifraga: Strawberry-geranium. Strawberry-begonia. Plain-leaved *S. stolonifera* and the white-rose-green *S. s. tricolor* are outstanding for terrarium plantings. Start with young, established plants. Closed. Cool to warm. Half sun to shade. Fluorescent light. Woodsy moist.

Scilla: The tender *S. violacea* is a beautiful foliage plant all year, with spikes of tiny flowers in season. Start with a young, established plant. In a terrarium it will multiply so that within a year you will have several, which may be left as one clump or divided. Closed or open. Warm. Half sun. Fluorescent light. Woodsy moist.

Scindapsus: Pothos. This trailing philodendronlike plant is often included in commercially planted terrariums and dish gardens. Rooted cuttings may be confined to a small space for a few weeks, or possibly months, but this is not an ideal terrarium plant. Closed or open. Warm. Half sun to shade. Fluorescent light. Woodsy moist.

Seemannia: A gesneriad, related to the African violet. Miniature to 6 inches tall with bright green leaves and orange-red flowers. May be nearly everblooming in a fluorescent-

ABOVE: Saxifraga stolonifera tricolor. *BELOW:* Scilla violacea.

ABOVE: Selaginella kraussiana. BELOW: Siderasis fuscata.

BELOW: Sinningia *(miniature gloxinia)*.

light garden. Closed. Warm. Fluorescent light. Woodsy moist.

Selaginella: Sweat plant (*S. emmeliana*), spreading club moss (*S. kraussiana*), dwarf club moss (*S. k. brownii*), and *S. uncinata* are among the best of all terrarium plants. Although miniature by nature, they tend to spread and even climb (in very high humidity), so that some pruning and training is necessary from time to time. Start with rooted cuttings or young, established plants. Closed. Warm. Shade. Fluorescent light. Woodsy moist.

Serissa: Small shrublet with dark green leaves and tiny white flowers. An interesting form for terrarium plantings, especially in combination with rocks. Start with an established, young plant or rooted cutting. Closed or open. Warm. Half sun to shade. Fluorescent light. Woodsy moist.

Siderasis: This relative of the wandering Jew forms low rosettes of furry leaves that are olive-green, silvery, and burgundy colored. From time to time there are lavender-blue flowers. Excellent in a fairly large terrarium. A tidy plant that only occasionally needs to have one of the older, yellowing leaves removed. Closed or open. Warm. Half sun to shade. Fluorescent light. Woodsy moist.

Sinningia: Gloxinia. *Sinningia pusilla,* the miniature gloxinia, and any of its hybrids, along with *S. concinna* and its offspring, are superb flowering plants for all kinds of terrarium plantings. You can even plant one of these in a 2-inch clear plastic cube for a miniature terrarium. They tend to be nearly everblooming. Start with established, young plants purchased from a specialist. Many of these seed themselves, eventually forming colonies of plants in a terrarium. Closed. Warm. Half sun to shade. Fluorescent light. Woodsy moist.

Smithiantha: Members of the gesneriad family, related to African violets and gloxinia. Beautiful foliage and breathtaking flowers in season. Too large except for a sizable terrarium. Closed. Warm. Half sun. Fluorescent light. Woodsy moist.

Sonerila: Delicate foliage plants with flowers in season. Excellent miniatures. Start with established, young plants. Closed. Warm. Half sun to shade. Fluorescent light. Woodsy moist.

Streptocarpus: A gesneriad, related to the African violet. Until recently most were too large for terrariums. However, recent hybrids like 'Mini-Nymph' and 'Netta Nymph' are excellent. They grow about a hand spread across and the flowering stems to 6 inches high. Start with young, established plants. Closed. Warm. Half sun. Fluorescent light. Woodsy moist.

Thymus: Thyme. Available in both creeping and upright forms. Start from seeds or purchase young, established plants. Shear back as necessary to maintain desired size and shape; use clippings for seasoning. Open. Cool to warm. Sunny. Fluorescent light. Woodsy moist to slightly dry.

Tillandsia: This genus of bromeliads contains many plants that may be enjoyed in a terrarium while they are young — and therefore small enough. There are also some that mature and flower as miniatures. Check with mail-order specialists in bromeliads to see what is currently available. Spanish moss, *T. usneoides,* is sometimes successfully cultivated in a terrarium that has high humidity. Closed. Warm. Half sun. Fluorescent light. Woodsy moist.

Tolmiea: Piggyback. Pickaback. This foliage plant grows much too large for most terrariums, but baby plants may be rooted and grown for some months in this manner. Closed. Cool to warm. Half sun to shade. Fluorescent light. Woodsy moist.

Tradescantia: Wandering Jew. A large grouping of foliage plants best cultivated as hanging baskets in open air. Tip cuttings root almost overnight in a terrarium and may be cultivated in this manner, but unless you constantly clip them back they will crowd out the other plants. Closed or open. Warm. Sunny to half sun. Fluorescent light. Woodsy moist.

Viola: Violet. *V. odorata,* the sweet violet, is fun to try in a terrarium. Transplant from your garden or purchase a young, established plant from a wildflower specialist (who may list other tiny violets you'd like to try — but stay away from larger kinds known popularly as violas and pansies). Closed or open. Cool. Half sun to shade. Fluorescent light. Woodsy moist.

Zebrina: Wandering Jew. See comments and culture for *Tradescantia* (also called wandering Jew).

ABOVE: Sonerila margaritacea argentea.

ABOVE: Miniature Tillandsia. *BELOW:* Tolmiea.

*A desertscape of miniature cacti and succulents planted in
an 8-inch diameter clay saucer.*

5
The Desert in Miniature

If cacti and other succulents appeal to you, try growing them in open terrariums, low dishes, trays, and pottery bowls. Keep in mind that as house plants most of them require full, direct sun for as many hours as possible each day. If you have no sunny windows, then a fluorescent-light garden can make a fairly successful substitute for the real thing.

Also remember that most of these containers have no drainage hole to allow the escape of excess water. Strive for a happy medium between dusty, bone dry (which is too dry even for desert plants) and wet.

The one problem you may have in planting cacti in any terrarium or dish garden is in handling the thorny bodies. The painless way is to take a sheet of newspaper and fold it over and over into a thick strip about 1 inch wide. Loop this around each cactus to lift, position, and hold it in place until the soil is firmed about the roots.

In the Little Encyclopedia of Desertscape Plants which follows, you will notice that each has the designation "Desert." This refers both to the composition of the planting medium and the amount of moisture it receives. Basic planting steps for a desertscape are the same as for an open terrarium (see Chapter 2). Instead of using packaged potting soil or special terrarium soil, purchase a kind labeled specifically for cacti and other desert succulents. Or mix 1 part *each* of packaged potting soil, peat moss, and perlite to 3 parts clean sharp sand.

Study all of Chapter 2, review the cacti and other succulents described and illustrated in this chapter, then proceed to create your own desert in miniature. The care of cacti and succulents is given in greater detail in *Cacti and Succulents* by William C. Mulligan, a Good Life Book, Grosset & Dunlap (1975).

ABOVE: Young aloe in flower.

ABOVE: Bishop's cap (Astrophytum). BELOW: Young Cereus cactus.

Little Encyclopedia of Desertscape Plants

Acanthocalycium: Globe cactus. Seedling or young plant. Open. Cool. Sunny. Desert.

Adromischus: Clustering succulents. Many with beautifully variegated foliage. Miniature or young plant. Open. Warm. Sunny. Fluorescent light. Desert.

Aeonium: Rosette-forming succulents. Some are naturally miniature; others can be used as young plants. Open. Warm. Half sun. Fluorescent light. Desert.

Agave: Century plant. Mostly giant rosettes of succulent leaves, but interesting subjects for containerized desertscapes while they are very young. Open. Warm. Sunny. Fluorescent light. Desert.

Aloe: Mostly large rosette-forming succulents useful in containerized desertscapes only as young plants. Open. Warm. Sunny. Fluorescent light. Desert.

Aloinopsis: Miniature succulent. Open. Warm. Sunny. Fluorescent light. Desert.

Anacampseros: Small succulents, often mat-forming. Rooted cuttings or young plants. Open. Warm. Sunny. Fluorescent light. Desert.

Apicra: Small succulents which may remind you of the better known aloe and haworthia. Use rooted cuttings or young plants. Open. Warm. Sunny to half sun. Fluorescent light. Desert.

Aptenia: Trailing succulent with gray and white heart-shaped leaves. The little flowers are purple. Rooted cuttings or young plants. Open. Warm. Sunny. Fluorescent light. Woodsy moist.

Argyroderma: Small, clustering succulents. Mostly of a miniature nature and excellent for containerized desertscapes. Open. Warm. Sunny. Fluorescent light. Desert.

Astrophytum: Sand dollar, bishop's cap, and other spherical succulents. Excellent for small desertscapes. Open. Warm. Sunny. Fluorescent light. Desert.

Beaucarnea: Pony-tail. Elephant's-foot. Succulent member of the lily family with a swollen base that protrudes above the soil line. Only seedlings or young plants are suited to containerized desertscapes as the *Beaucarnea*

A desert microcosm, this fishtank planting of cacti/succulents receives supplementary night light from a table lamp.

grows eventually to giant size. Open. Warm. Sunny. Fluorescent light. Desert.

Cheiridopsis: Clustering, mat-forming, or tufting succulents. Open. Warm. Sunny. Fluorescent light. Desert.

Conophytum: Miniature succulent bodies. Open. Warm. Sunny. Fluorescent light. Desert.

Coryphantha: Globe cactus. Open. Warm. Sunny. Fluorescent light. Desert.

Crassula: Jade plant. Creepers to low uprights to tree form jade plant (*C. argentea*). There are dozens of different crassulas; in fact, you might create an entire containerized des-

ertscape using only these succulents. Use seedlings, rooted cuttings, or young plants. Open. Warm. Sunny. Fluorescent light. Desert.

Delosperma: Mostly small-growing succulents. Start with rooted cuttings or young plants. Open. Warm. Sunny. Fluorescent light. Desert.

Echeveria: Succulent relatives of the crassula. Seedlings and rooted cuttings of almost all make interesting subjects for containerized desertscapes. Open. Warm. Sunny. Fluorescent light. Desert.

Echinocereus: Globe and other growth

ABOVE: Crassula tetragona. *BELOW:* Crassula argentea (*jade plant*).

shapes associated with cacti. Seedlings and rooted cuttings are useful in small desertscapes. Open. Warm. Sunny. Fluorescent light. Desert.

Echinofossulocactus: Unusual members of the cactus family. Seedlings and rooted cuttings may be used in desertscapes. Open. Warm. Sunny. Fluorescent light. Desert.

Euphorbia: Christmas poinsettia. The Christmas poinsettia is *E. pulcherrima,* but it is like the tip of an iceberg for this genus includes hundreds of fascinating succulents for containerized desertscapes. Most grow large eventually, but not before you have had years of pleasure from them. Study catalogs of cacti/succulent specialists. Start with seedlings, rooted cuttings, or young plants. Open. Warm. Sunny. Fluorescent light. Desert.

Fenestraria: Baby toes. Clustering, tufting succulents. Start with seedlings, rooted cuttings, or young plants. Open. Warm. Sunny. Fluorescent light. Desert.

Frithia: Purple baby toes. Clustered, windowed succulent. Open. Warm. Sunny. Fluorescent light. Desert.

Gasteria: Fairly large group of succulents worthy of cultivating for their handsome foliage. Start with seedlings, rooted cuttings, or young plants. Open. Warm. Half sun. Fluorescent light. Desert.

Gibbaeum: Cluster-forming succulent bodies. Start with seedlings or young plants. Open. Warm. Sunny. Fluorescent light. Desert.

Graptopetalum: Ghost plant. Interesting succulent with rosettes of silvery white leaves. Start with rooted cuttings or young plants. Open. Warm. Sunny. Fluorescent light. Desert.

Greenovia: Rosettes of blue-green succulent leaves; related to the crassula. Start with rooted cuttings or young plants. Open. Warm. Sunny. Fluorescent light. Desert.

Gymnocalycium: Globe cactus. Outstanding for desertscaping in containers. Start with seedlings or young plants. Open. Warm. Sunny. Fluorescent light. Desert.

Haworthia: A large group of rosette-forming succulents of the lily family. Start with seedlings, rooted cuttings, or young plants. Open. Warm. Half sun. Fluorescent light. Desert.

Huernia: Fascinating small succulents.

Barrel cactus (Echinocactus grusonii).

Gymnocalycium delaetii.

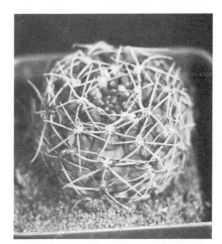

Gymnocalycium leeanum.

Gymnocalycium denudatum.

Gymnocalycium quehlianum.

ABOVE: Lithops in flower.

BELOW LEFT: Kleinia articulatus.

Lithops in tray garden.

Start with seedlings, rooted cuttings, or young plants. Open. Warm. Half sun. Fluorescent light. Desert.

Kalanchoe: A large genus of interesting succulents for containerized desertscapes. Some grow small naturally, others can be kept reasonably small by pruning. Start with seedlings, rooted cuttings, or young plants. Open. Warm. Sunny. Fluorescent light. Desert.

Kleinia: Succulent members of the daisy family. Start with rooted cuttings or young plants. Open. Warm. Sunny. Fluorescent light. Desert.

Lampranthus: Succulent creepers, mostly with gray-green leaves and many with showy flowers in season. Open. Warm. Sunny. Fluorescent light. Desert.

Lithops: Stoneface. Living stone. Miniature succulents. Hundreds of different kinds are in cultivation. They are superb for small desertscapes. Start with seeds, seedlings, or young plants. Open. Warm. Sunny. Fluorescent light. Desert.

Lobivia: Globe cactus. Some naturally small, others suited to a small desertscape only while young. Start with seedlings or young plants. Open. Warm. Sunny. Fluorescent light. Desert.

Mammillaria: A vast grouping of succulents from the cactus family. Start with seeds, seedlings, rooted cuttings, or young plants. Open. Cool to warm. Sunny. Fluorescent light. Desert.

Melocactus: Globe or turk's cap cactus. Start with young plants. Open. Warm. Sunny. Fluorescent light. Desert.

Monanthes: Miniature succulents. Start with young plants. Open. Warm. Sunny. Fluorescent light. Desert.

Nananthus: Miniature succulents. Start with young, established plants. Open. Warm. Sunny. Fluorescent light. Desert.

Notocactus: Globe cactus. Some naturally small, others grow large with age. All are useful while young in desertscapes. Start with seedlings or young, established plants. Open. Cool to warm. Sunny. Fluorescent light. Desert.

Opuntia: Prickly-pear. Pad cactus. Mostly large succulents, but useful in containerized

ABOVE: Mammillaria euthele.

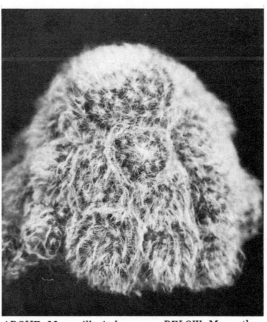

ABOVE: Mammillaria bocasana. *BELOW:* Monanthes.

Opuntia vistata.

Senecio haworthii.

desertscapes while young. Open. Warm. Sunny. Fluorescent light (only while quite small). Desert.

Pachyphytum: Beautiful foliage succulents related to the crassulas. Start with rooted cuttings or young, established plants. Open. Warm. Sunny. Fluorescent light. Desert.

Pachyveria: Hybrid succulents resulting from crosses of *Pachyphytum* and *Echeveria*. Young plants excellent for desertscapes. Open. Warm. Sunny. Fluorescent light. Desert.

Parodia: Globe cactus. Small-growing and excellent for desertscapes. Start with young plants. Open. Warm. Sunny. Fluorescent light. Desert.

Pleiospilos: Mimicry plant. Fascinating miniature succulents. Start with young established plants. Open. Warm. Sunny. Fluorescent light. Desert.

Portulacaria: Elephant bush. Young plants are easily shaped and trained to give the appearance of desert shrubs in miniature. In fact, this succulent is often used as a bonsai. Start with a young, established plant or rooted cutting. Open. Warm. Sunny. Fluorescent light. Desert.

Rebutia: Clustering miniature cacti. Outstanding for containerized desertscapes. Start with seeds, seedlings, or young, established plants. Open. Cool to warm. Sunny. Fluorescent light. Desert.

Sedum: This group of succulents is rich in materials for desertscapes of almost all sizes. Start with rooted cuttings or young, established plants. Open. Warm. Sunny. Fluorescent light. Desert.

Sempervivum: Hen-and-chicks. Houseleek. Rosette-forming succulents of many sizes and colors for desertscapes. Open. Cool to warm. Sunny. Desert.

Senecio: This genus includes the popular florist gift plant, cineraria, but there are several succulent types you may find in the catalogs of cacti/succulent specialists. Start with rooted cuttings or young, established plants. Open. Warm. Sunny. Fluorescent light. Desert.

Stapelia: Clambering or spreading succulents with star-shaped flowers that give off a foul odor. Interesting addition to a fairly large containerized desertscape, preferably one that can be kept out of doors most of the year. Open. Warm. Sunny. Desert.

Titanopsis: Miniature succulents. Start with young, established plants. Open. Warm. Sunny. Fluorescent light. Desert.

Spiraling array of different sempervivums (in tray garden with marble chip mulch) emphasizes their beauty.

6
Carnivorous Plants, Aquariums, Vivariums

Three kinds of miniature, glassed-in gardens are suggested in this chapter: terrariums of carnivorous plants, aquariums with underwater plants, and vivariums that combine plants with pets. Actually, they appeal to persons of all ages, but especially to children. They make great classroom projects, but each or all may be enjoyed even more when pursued together by an adult and a child at home.

Carnivorous Plants

Insect-eating plants are truly among the most fascinating of all living things. A closed terrarium is the only feasible way to cultivate these plants as house plants, and even then most need coolness in winter. Children can catch small live insects and place them inside the terrarium. Slowly the plants go into action, enticing and trapping the unsuspecting victims.

The list that follows includes all of the carnivorous plants commonly available and suited to terrarium culture. It is best to obtain these from specialists, not as the highly commercialized packaged products sometimes offered by mail-order houses of questionable repute.

Pinguicula: Butterwort. Carnivorous. Miniature. Start with established, young plants. Closed. Cool to warm. Shade. Fluorescent light. Woodsy wet.

Darlingtonia: Cobra Plant. Carnivorous. Strange hooded growth. Not beautiful in the usual sense but truly fascinating. Start with a young, established plant obtained from a specialist. Closed. Cool. Shade. Fluorescent light. Woodsy moist to wet.

Sarracenia: Pitcher plant. Huntsman's horn. Carnivorous. Purchase young, established plant from wildflower specialist. Closed or open. Cool. Sunny to half sun. Fluorescent light. Woodsy with unmilled sphagnum moss and wet.

Drosera: Sundew. Carnivorous. Various miniatures, all fascinating to watch in a terrarium. Start with young, established plants. Closed. Cool. Fluorescent light. Woodsy wet.

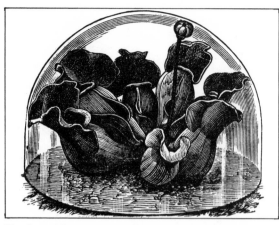

Woodcut of Sarracenia *(pitcher plant).*

Dionaea: Venus's-flytrap. Carnivorous. Miniature rosettes of spoon-shaped leaves with long teeth along the edges. If a fly stays too long on the leaf surface, it will fold together

Woodcut of Dionaea *(Venus's-flytrap).*

with the teeth interlocking like fingers clasped. Start with a young, established plant. Closed. Cool. Fluorescent light. Moist to wet unmilled sphagnum moss.

Aquarium Plants (with or without Fish)

The prettiest fresh-water aquariums with the healthiest fish are usually those well planted with aquatic plants. Some are surprisingly beautiful. Specialists stock a variety of suitable plants, but some you are likely to find

include anacharis (or elodea), eichornia, and vallisneria. Anchor the roots of these plants in an ample mound of coarse sand.

Underwater plants require relatively little light in order to thrive. A medium size aquarium with one 15- or 20-watt fluorescent over it will grow a fascinating collection of thriving aquatic plants.

Anacharis: Water-thyme. An excellent plant for the spawn of fish. The stems are covered with small leaves not unlike those of culinary thyme although the two plants are not related. Submerge in water.

Cabomba: Fanwort. Fans of threadlike leaves, reminiscent of dill foliage. Delicate in appearance but easily cultivated. One of the best oxygenators and widely distributed. Grows quickly and the color is a bright, refreshing green. Submerge in water.

Echinodorus: Amazon sword plant. Bright green spear-shaped leaves spread out in fans. Bold, tropical appearance. Submerge in water.

Hydrocleys: Water-poppy. This small plant floats on the surface of the water and produces lovely poppylike flowers in season. *H. commersonii* is the species most often cultivated in aquariums. Plant roots in a pocket of soil submerged in water.

Hygrophila: Pale green leaves have silvery undersides. Cuttings root easily. Not as well known as most other aquarium plants, but certainly worth growing. Submerge in water.

Ludwigia: This aquatic plant has rounded red and green leaves. Although it grows mostly submerged, some of the leaves will appear on the surface of the water, and in sunlight these turn coppery and red.

Myriophyllum: Two species of this plant are commonly cultivated in aquariums. *M. proserpinacoides* is almost always called parrot's feather with reference to the feathery light green leaves that grow in whorls about the stems which tend to grow out of the water and cascade attractively from the container. *M. heterophyllum* (and sometimes *M. pinnatum* and *M. rubrifolium*), also called water-milfoil, resembles cabomba but is more delicate in appearance. An excellent oxygenator. Submerge in water.

Plants submerged in water make a fascinating aquascape in this crystal temple jar.

Vivariums:
Plants and Pets Together

Mostly this book is about plants and people living together; now we add the possibility of including such creatures as chameleons, frogs, toads, and salamanders to a terrarium with a fine screened covering.

A standard rectangular fish aquarium makes an ideal container for a vivarium. At the pet store, where you can also purchase the aquarium, you will find suitable animals to place inside it. What you want to create is a natural home for the animals so that both you and they will not think of them as caged but rather in a hospitable habitat.

Before you place different kinds of animals in the vivarium, be sure that they are compatible. Generally speaking, frogs of the same size can be placed together with toads of the same size and turtles. Geckos of the same size may be placed together, along with lizards. Most lizards may be placed with other lizards of the same size and turtles. The common chameleon is compatible with horned toads.

Salamanders of the same size may be housed together, along with small frogs. Skinks and small lizards are acceptable companions. Place toads of the same size together or with lizards. Turtles do well together and with lizards.

What to Feed Your Pets

When you purchase the animals for your vivarium, ask the shopkeeper for advice about diet, care, and handling. The following suggestions will give you a general idea of what to expect.

Chameleons: Small grasshoppers, houseflies, mosquitoes, caterpillars, fruit flies, meal worms (available at your pet shop). As with the terrarium of carnivorous plants, children will often be interested in catching their food. Provide water by dropping it onto the leaves of plants.

Frogs and Toads: Cockroaches, grasshoppers, worms, plant insects (aphids, for example). Provide land and water in the vivarium.

Salamanders and Newts: Plant insects (aphids, mealybugs, for example) and worms. Provide land and water, preferably with a kind of diving-board rock jutting out over the water.

Geckos: Meal worms or live insects. Supplement this diet with a mixture of equal parts cod liver oil, honey, molasses, and a little orange juice. Provide dry land and water.

Lizards: Ants and small insects, also plant leaves. Provide a terrain that is mostly sandy and dry; stones and rocks are to their liking.

Skinks: Insect larvae, worms, grubs. Provide dry land and water.

Turtles: Best choices are land turtles or land/water turtles. Provide dry land and water. Change the water often enough to keep it clean and clear. Some turtles carry the disease salmonellosis; so it is best to purchase them with a guarantee that they are disease free. Wash hands after handling. It is a good idea not to pet them anyway — for your sake and theirs. Most turtles will eat very small bits of *raw* chicken or lean beef; also meal worms and earthworms as well as bits of carrots, lettuce, and fresh fruit. They also eat plants.

As you plan and plant your vivarium, be sure to leave plenty of open space so that the animals can move about freely.

Vivarium container with screen top and light.

A large clay saucer has been used to contain this planting of tufting Alpine dianthus, Draba species and small-growing species Sedum *and* Sempervivum. *Various unusual rocks complete this interesting scene.*

7
How to Grow
Your Own Alpine Meadow

I must be forthright and tell you that most of these plants will not survive outdoor climates that are hot and dry in the summer; nor can they survive year round residence in a centrally heated house or apartment. Where winter temperatures dip more than a few degrees below freezing, they need to be protected in a cold frame or brought along in a cool sun-heated pit. If you haven't already given up and turned the page, let me add that an increasing number of northern gardeners are successfully cultivating these plants in shallow trays, troughs, and large clay pots.

In essence what we have here are plants with which to create miniature open terrariums to be cultivated like most bonsai, largely out of doors. In hot summer weather they need a cool, moist, shaded spot. In early spring and late fall you can move them into more direct sun.

Wintering-over in cold climates can be done in a well-insulated cold frame, in a cool to cold sun-heated pit, or under fluorescent lights in a cool room (perhaps you have a guest room or sun porch that does not need to have the heating unit turned on during most of the winter). For planting ideas and the ways and means of caring for these plants, study the accompanying photographs and captions. Suggested plant materials follow in lists divided according to types. Sources are listed in Appendix A, and as most of these plants must come from special nurseries by mail, instructions will be sent with the plants or appear in the catalogs.

Alpine Garden Flowers

Latin Name	Common Name
Anagallis tenella	Bog pimpernel
Arenaria balearica	
Asperula suberosa	
Astilbe glaberrima 'Saxosa'	
Campanula cochlearifolia	Bellflower
C. pulla	Bellflower
Centaurium portense	
Dianthus musalae	Pink
D. myrtinervis	Pink
D. 'Prince Charming'	Pink
Douglasia vitaliana	
Draba aizoides	
D. imbricata	
Erinus alpinus	
Erodium chamaedry-oides roseum	
Frankenia laevis	Sea heath
Gentiana verna	Spring gentian
Helianthemum alpestre	Miniature sun-rose
Hypericum anagalloides	St. John's-wort
Hypsella longiflora	
Limonium minutum	Miniature sea lavender
Linaria alpina	Alpine Toadflax
Linnaea borealis	Twinflower
Lobelia linnaeoides	
Myosotis rupicola	Miniature forget-me-not
Phlox douglasii 'Eva'	
Pimelia coarctata	Rice plant
Potentilla verna pygmaea	
Primula frondosa	Primrose
P. scotica	Primrose
Raoulia australis	
R. glabra	
R. lutescens	
Saxifraga burseriana 'Gloria'	
S. 'Cranbourne'	
S. 'Faldonside'	
S. irvingii	
Sedum dasyphyllum	Live forever
S. farinosum	Live forever
S. humifusum	Live forever
Sempervivum arach-noideum	Houseleek
S. arenarium	Houseleek
Sibthorpia europaea var-iegata	Cornish moneywort
Soldanella alpina	
Veronica telephiifolia	
Viola hederacea	Australian violet

Alpine Garden Shrubs

Latin Name	Common Name
Cassiope lycopodioides	
C. tetragona	
Corokia cotoneaster	
Erica vulgaris foxii nana	Miniature heather
Grevillea alpina	Alpine silk-oak
Helichrysum selago mi-nor	Everlasting
Jasminum parkeri	Miniature jasmine
Leiophyllum buxifolium	
Leptospermum scopar-ium prostratum	
Rhododendron species	Dwarf rhododendron and azalea
Rosa roulettii hybrids	Miniature rose
Salix boydii	Willow
S. herbacea	Willow
S. retusa pyrenaica	Willow
S. serpyllifolia	Willow
Ulmus parvifolia 'Ches-sins'	Miniature elm
Zelkova nivea	Miniature Japanese elm

Alpine Evergreens (Conifers)

Latin Name	Common Name
Chamaecyparis lawsoniana 'Elwoodii'	Cypress
C. l. 'Minima Aurea'	Cypress
C. obtusa 'Nana'	Cypress
C. o. 'Nana Caespitosa'	Cypress
C. o. 'Nana Flabelliformis'	Cypress
C. o. 'Nana Juniperoides'	Cypress
C. o. 'Nana Kosterii'	Cypress
C. o. 'Tetragona Aurea'	Cypress
C. pisifera 'Boulevard'	Cypress
C. p. 'Nana'	Cypress
C. p. 'Plumosa Aurea Compacta'	Cypress
C. p. 'Squarrosa	

Intermedia'	Cypress
C. thyoides 'Andeleyensis'	Cypress
Cryptomeria japonica 'Vilmoriniana'	
Juniperus communis 'Compressa'	Juniper
J. c. 'Echinoformis'	Hedgehog juniper
J. procumbens 'Nana'	Juniper
J. scopulorum 'Repens'	Prostrate juniper
J. squamata 'Wilsonii'	Juniper
Microcachrys tetragona	
Picea abies 'Clanbrassiliana'	Norway spruce
P. albertiana 'Conica'	Spruce
P. mariana 'Nana'	Spruce
Thuja orientalis 'Rosedalis'	Arborvitae

Alpine Water Garden Plants

Latin Name	Common Name
Azolla caroliniana	Fairy Moss
Hydrocharis morsus-ranae	Frog-bit

Miniature rose 'Easter Morning' in a 4-inch pot.

Aubrieta deltoides, *spring-flowering Alpine.*

ABOVE: These Japanese maple seedlings have been carefully arranged in a redwood tray and trained, bonsai-style,
to represent woody growth of an Alpine meadow.

OPPOSITE: This Zelkova species, the true Japanese elm,
has been dwarfed by bonsai techniques, to represent an Alpine meadow specimen.

OPPOSITE, ABOVE: This is a midwinter scene inside the sun-heated pit greenhouse of Mr. and Mrs. Lucien B. Taylor, who reside in the Northeast. Inside they grow many Alpine plants along with camellias, acacia, daffodils, crocus, and hyacinths.

OPPOSITE, BELOW: This exterior view of the Taylors' sun-heated pit shows how the glass sashes are slanted toward the south to catch full benefit of the sun's rays. The opposite side of the roof is heavily insulated and shingled to protect from cold north winds. At night and on cloudy days during the winter plastic foam pads are placed over the glass to keep the heat inside. No heat, other than that provided by solar energy, is used to warm the greenhouse. Note also that the door is thick and insulated. Steps lead down into the pit which is approximately 4 feet deep. Kathryn Taylor, along with Edith Gregg, has written a book called **Winter Flowers** *in Greenhouse and Sun-Heated Pit (Scribner's).*

ABOVE: Mrs. Taylor grows countless rare wild flowers from seeds in her sun-heated pit. The plants in this photograph are various species of Viola; *note in particular the double flowers on the center plant, a treasured, sweet-scented violet.*

RIGHT: This small shrub, Daphne odora, *does especially well when wintered in a sun-heated pit. In late winter and early spring it bears intensely fragrant flowers.*

*In a large terrarium or Wardian case it is possible to grow
exotic tropicals like this showy* Calathea.

8
Window Greenhouses, Wardian Cases, and Enclosed Light Gardens

You'll find on the market today a variety of large glass or plastic enclosures for growing plants. Some depend on natural light, others come equipped with fluorescent fixtures.

Table-top greenhouses are really just modern-day versions of Victorian Wardian cases. One presently on the market, available both by mail and through department and garden stores, measures 18 inches deep, 15 inches high, and 24 inches wide. The frame is made of masonite and it has 22 windows of clear plastic. One side of the roof swings open for easy access to the plants and to allow for ventilation and humidity control. This unit might be used in natural light, or a fluorescent reflector fixture with two 20-watt tubes might be suspended over it.

You can also build a table-top greenhouse, using strips of redwood for the framing and either glass, Plexiglas, or Lucite for the windows.

Inside a table-top greenhouse you can set it up as a replica in miniature of a working greenhouse, complete with benches, a narrow walkway, and thumb pots of Lilliputian plants. Add diminutive hanging baskets of tiny creepers and vines to complete the picture.

Or, you can plant the entire table-top greenhouse as a miniature landscape, the theme for which might be Japanese, complete with a footbridge, tiny stone lanterns, and a meandering stream; or an English perennial border with clumps and tufts of leafy, grassy, and flowering plants; or a woodland dell with ferns, mosses, lichen, bits of weathered bark, and some lofty trees reaching toward the greenhouse roof.

Prefabricated window greenhouses vary from small units that extend out from the window, and are installed in the same manner as an air-conditioning unit, to larger window greenhouse units, designed to cover — or extend slightly beyond — an entire window, with one or more shelves on which you can display a number of terrariums. In north light these can be open or closed; if the window greenhouse receives direct sun, place only open terrariums inside. The space inside one of these is excellent for planting a miniature landscape. Select plants according to the amount of light the window greenhouse receives.

An empty aquarium with a 20-watt fluorescent placed over it and burned 14 hours daily, makes a propagator.

Decorative fluorescent unit with one 20-watt tube.

One of the most recent introductions to home greenhouses is a greenhouse terrarium 60 inches tall, 39 inches wide, and 20 inches deep. It has a white plastic frame, clear plastic covering, and a door for easy access to the two shelves inside. In this unit you might grow any number of terrariums, open or closed in north light, open if the unit receives direct sun.

In the accompanying illustrations you will also see several kinds of growth chambers, which come equipped with fluorescent light fixtures. Although the humidity inside these is too high for most cacti and other desert succulents, you can grow almost any other terrarium plants in them. These units give you complete control over all growth factors except temperature; inside these closed units with the fluorescent lights burning, temperatures are approximately 10 degrees higher than the room in which they are placed. In the average home

This plastic-covered greenhouse, designed to be placed in-doors in a sunny window, makes a large terrarium.

The Plantarium shown on these pages is available with or without fluorescent lighting.

ABOVE: African violets and Dracaena godseffiana 'Florida Beauty' thrive in the warmth and high humidity assured by this kind of growth chamber. These plants would thrive in a bright east or west window, or in a southern exposure with noonday shading.

LEFT: The same Plantarium unit is shown here planted as a large-scale terrarium with rocks, a pool of water and the soil formed into a fascinating landscape design. The plants include (from left to right) aluminum plant, aphelandra, rex begonia, maidenhair fern, and a flowering episcia.

OPPOSITE: With the addition of a fluorescent fixture with two 40-watt tubes burned 14 hours out of every 24, the Plantarium can be used to nurture flowering and foliage plants in a dark corner or hallway where no natural light reaches.

Fluorescent-lighted china cabinet holds rare plants.

this means that they are ideally suited to tropical foliage and flowering plants such as African violets, episcias, miniature gloxinias, calatheas, marantas, rex begonias, and certain exquisite orchids (any referred to as "jewel orchids").

If you have a full-scale home greenhouse, terrariums of all kinds can be cultivated to perfection. Situate the closed ones in shade; provide an appropriate amount of direct sun, depending on the kinds of plants you are growing, for the open terrariums. A home greenhouse is also a potential gold mine for propagating hundreds of different terrarium plants. One home greenhouse gardener of my acquaintance, Sandra Mauro, brings classes of school children into her greenhouse and teaches them how to make cuttings, then how to plant terrariums and bottle gardens. She uses gallon-size pickle and mayonnaise jars because they are available at no charge from commercial kitchens and the large openings make planting relatively easy for youngsters.

A greenhouse is ideal for growing miniature gardens.

Fluorescent light illuminates terrarium in a fireplace.

Miniature orchids like these cattleya hybrids will thrive in a terrarium that receives some fresh air.

*The arrow points to the telltale spots of powdery mildew on
begonia leaves; fresh air helps avoid mildew.*

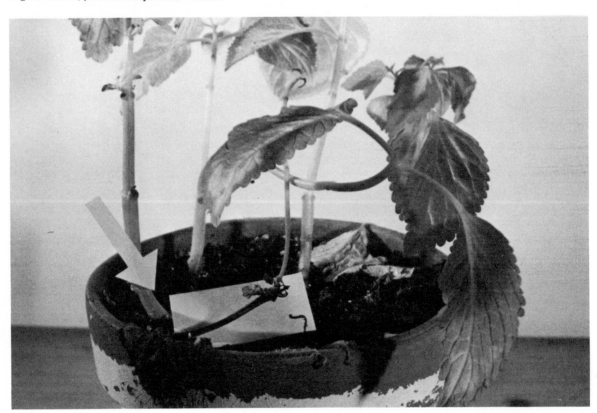

*Arrow points to coleus leaves and stems that have rotted for
lack of air circulation.*

9
Terrarium Trouble Signs – and What to Do

If you do your homework well, more often than not a terrarium will be the most trouble-free of all gardening endeavors. However, just in case something goes wrong, here are some fairly common symptoms and suggestions for what to do about them.

Plants Tall, Lanky, Weak-Stemmed; Leaves Frail or Pale: The terrarium needs more light. The plants you are trying to grow may need more fresh air, or less water. Take this problem firmly in hand. Start over, either by removing all plants and cutting them back or by purchasing compact new ones.

Walls of Container Constantly Fogged Over Entirely with Moisture: Too much water inside. Remove cork or cover until walls are clear, then replace. If they quickly cloud over again, repeat the same procedure. Do this until they remain mostly clear, but not entirely. It is healthy for some moisture to condense on the walls and trickle back into the soil.

Leaves Wilt and Develop Yellow or Brown, Burned Spots: Too much hot sun shining directly through the walls of the terrarium onto tender leaves. Reduce amount of sun or switch to a fluorescent-light garden.

Leaves Wilt or Look Pale; Moss Ground Cover Turns Pale or Brown: The terrarium is too dry. Add a little water and mist the foliage with an atomizer.

Water Stands on Surface of the Soil; Soil and Plants Floating on Water: You've watered too much. To solve this problem in an open terrarium, take a bulb baster and draw off the excess water. In a closed terrarium, such as a bottle garden, you may find it necessary to siphon off the water by using a length of small rubber or plastic tubing.

Insects Visible on Leaves and Stems: Cut off an inch-long piece of a Shell No-Pest Strip and place it inside the terrarium. (Fumes given off by the strip [Vapona is the chemical] will kill the bugs.) In an open terrarium you can treat insect pests by mixing a liquid house-plant pesticide in a small atomizer or plant mister; line the inside walls of the terrarium with paper toweling, then carefully spray the infested plants. Under no circumstance should you spray an aerosol of houseplant pesticide inside a terrarium; it will coat the walls with an oily residue that is difficult to remove.

Leaves or Stems Rotted Off; Mold or Mildew Forms. Too much moisture; lack of air circulation. Some plants are not suited to a terrarium that is always

Arrow points to worm that has been chewing leaves.

Brown scale can be removed with tip of knife blade.

closed. Angel-wing and semperflorens begonias, for example, will quickly develop powdery mildew in such a container.

Leaves and Stems Fill the Terrarium in a Tangled Mass of Undefined Growth: Complete replanting is in order. Completely clean out the terrarium and start over from Step 1, which is to wash it in warm soapy water, rinse, and dry. Use fresh gravel, charcoal, and potting soil. Cut back old plants, make cuttings of them (which may be rooted directly in the terrarium), or use new plants.

One Plant is Growing Rampantly, Climbing Over and Crowding Out the Others: Cut it back drastically, or remove entirely and replace with a better choice.

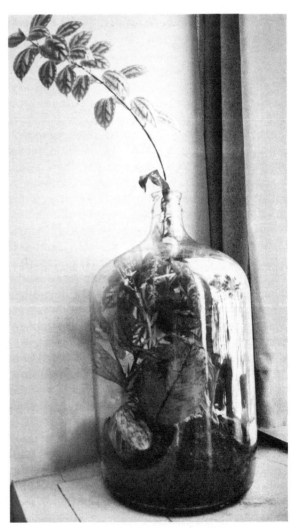

This bottle garden is badly in need of replanting.